Advance praise for thoughtware

"After helping AT&T units win three Baldrige Awards, a Deming Prize, two Shingo Prizes, and several state quality awards, I have finally found an approach for quality reorganizations to avoid major quality setbacks each time we reorganize. *Thoughtware* is a must read for every manager who is tired of starting all over again after every reorganization."

— Phil Scanlan, Quality Office Vice President
AT&T

"I have worked closely with the Thoughtware group. It is stimulating to see the new thought process so clearly articulated. This is a well conceptualized process that works."

— Ben R. Yorks, retired President and COO
ABC Rail Products Corporation

"Phil Kirby re-taught us how to think, only this time by adding creativity, a clean sheet approach, and a process perspective. Then he took us by the hand and showed us the way to implementation. Our investment in Phil and his company, Organizational Thoughtware, has been the most impactful investment we have ever made relative to our bottom line."

— Mike Klonne, President
Ato Findley, Inc.

"Phil Kirby and Organization Thoughtware, Inc. laid the groundwork for Piquniq Management Corporation's several diverse business units to begin discussions on improving communications. Our people defined common and unique processes on which to build better relationships leading to reductions in costs and time. Thanks!"

—CHARLES BROWER, PRESIDENT & CEO
PIQUNIQ MANAGEMENT CORPORATION

"If change is on your organizations agenda, then reading *Thoughtware* should be high on your list. This is not so much a management book as it is a navigational chart for the whole organization."

—CHARLES ARMSTRONG, PRESIDENT
S.A. ARMSTRONG LIMITED

"*Thoughtware* is a must read for any organizational leader serious about enhancing the capacity of his or her organization to compete successfully in the 21st century."

—TERRY MOORE, VICE PRESIDENT CORPORATE SERVICES
ALBERTA POWER LIMITED

thoughtware

J. Philip Kirby and David Hughes

thoughtware

*change the thinking
and the organization
will change itself*

Productivity Press
Portland, Oregon

Additional copies of this book are available from the publisher. Discounts are available for multiple copies through the Sales Department (800-394-6868). Address all other inquiries to:

Productivity Press
P.O. Box 13390
Portland OR 97213-0390
United States of America
Telephone: 503-235-0600
Telefax: 503-235-0909
E-mail: service@ppress.com

Cover illustration and text design by Bill Stanton
Photography by Barry Kaplan
Page composition by William H. Brunson Typography Services
Printed and bound by Edward Brothers in the United States of America

Library of Congress Cataloging-in-Publication Data

Kirby, J. Philip
    Thoughtware : change the thinking and the organization will change
itself / J. Philip Kirby and David Hughes.
        p. cm.
    Includes bibliographical references (p.).
    ISBN 1-56327-106-0 (hardcover)
    1. Organizational change. 2. Organizational behavior.
I. Hughes, David, 1942– . II. Title.
HD58.8.K518 1997
658.4′063—dc21   97-13605
                                                                     CIP

02 01 00 99 98 97 10 9 8 7 6 5 4 3 2 1

To my wife, Karen;
my children, Dylan, Emily, Rachel, and Brendan;
and my mother and father.

J. Philip Kirby

To my wife, Frances;
my children, Todd, Heather, and Ryan;
and in memory of my mother and father.

David Hughes

Table of Contents

PART TWO: NEW THOUGHTWARE

PART THREE: INSTALLATION

Publisher's Message

The failure of reengineering points to a fundamental misunderstanding of the process revolution initiated by the Toyota Production System. The continuous improvement methods of just-in-time, total quality control, and total productivity maintenance have given rise to a wave of questioning about the organizational mental models most of us hold, whether managers or staff or factory workers. The power of reengineering lies in its focus on process and cross-functionalism. However, these cannot take hold in an organization bound by mental models dependent on a single point of authority, limited span of control, and the perception of employees as costs rather than assets. Without addressing this underlying context, most reengineering efforts became a process of eliminating people to reduce costs rather than reducing process redundancies to expand capacity.

In *Thoughtware: Change the Thinking and The Organization Will Change Itself,* J. Philip Kirby and David Hughes lay out the limitations of the current context of thinking and describe the powerful elements of "new thoughtware" that are driving the process revolution and that comprise the foundation of the emerging era of knowledge management. It is critical to understand that the knowledge era is not fundamentally about technology, though technological innovation in telecommunications may be an enabling factor in its emergence. The new context we find ourselves a part of has arisen from a completely different understanding about how to work together and how to unleash the power of organized human effort. Kirby and Hughes have brilliantly articulated the features of this new context, the drivers and fundamental truths behind it, and a road map for installing the new thoughtware.

I first met David Hughes when we published a book written by his colleagues Patrick Northey and Nigel Southway *Cycle Time Management*. At that time, David and I spoke at length about emerging patterns in organizations and I was not surprised when several years later he approached me with this new manuscript and introduced me to Philip Kirby. Throughout our interactions, as we worked together to structure and refine their material, it was clear to me that we were mining gold. Kirby—charismatic and thorough, energetic and thoughtful—had enough material to write for years, and he kept moving on to discover new veins of pure ore deeper in the mine of his multi-dimensional perspective. David, with the reader ever at the forefront of his mind, continually asked questions to penetrate into the benefits of each new idea raised, and kept our ideas centered on the goal of a final manuscript. Meanwhile, I seemed to circle around them, weaving the threads of thought and structuring the ideas that flowed, working for consistency in the new terminology and to highlight the underlying patterns that shape the book.

Our work together has resulted in a book in which we take great pride. In Part One, the authors describe the elements of the old context comprised of the thoughtware of mass production—division of labor, departmentalization, limited span of control, and concentrated point of authority. This "old" thoughtware satisfied the needs of the industrial era, but today hinders an organization's flexibility and survival in an age where knowledge has become the primary commodity. In this first section, the authors explore the drivers of new context that challenge our understanding of how organizations should be structured. They also explore some basic truths inherent in the methods of continuous improvement and reengineering that are forcing an examination of the mental models at the base of our organizations. In Part Two, the elements of the new thoughtware—knowledge of the whole, measurement of what matters, a focus on time to action, and allowment (distributed points of authority)—are defined and thoroughly discussed. Part Three describes a methodology for installing the new thoughtware. Readers are to be cautioned, however, that this installation methodology is not another training program. It requires discipline and a capacity for self-examination. The authors offer a direction to a new way to manage and a pathway that aligns an organization with its future.

With this book, Productivity Press continues to serve our commitment to provide effective support for educating you and your workforce in methods that make a difference. For the last fifteen years we have brought to our readers the powerful methods of continuous improvement developed in Japanese factories, and more recently have been exploring the adaptation of these methods in North American and European factory environments. Now, in this book, we offer an in-depth clarification of the significant understanding underlying these methods and that must be in place in your organization for any of them to succeed. The new thoughtware described so beautifully in this book will make you fast, flexible, and powerfully focused on the future. It will become the operating platform to carry you successfully into the 21st century.

We are grateful to the authors for choosing Productivity Press as their publisher. In addition we wish to thank

Gary Peurasaari for his help in the development phases of the project, Elizabeth MacDonell for copyediting, Marvin Moore for proofreading, Mary Junewick for her tireless efforts in managing and executing the pre-press process, Bill Stanton for his brilliant cover and text designs, Bill Brunson for typesetting, and Edwards Brothers for printing and binding.

Diane Asay
Editor in Chief

Steven Ott
President and Publisher

Acknowledgments

Ackowledgments and "thank yous" can be like Academy Award speeches, too long and irrelevant for the audience, and yet, there is always a long list of people who should be thanked for their contribution to the thinking, writing, and publishing of a book. We've opted for relevance and a short list.

Thanks to all those insightful thinkers with whom we have worked over the years—colleagues, clients, friends, and family. A special thanks to Diane Asay, our editor, who has always seen the strength and merit of our work and been indispensible in leading the transformation of our thinking into a published book. And thanks to all those at Productivity Press who have helped in that painstaking process.

Finally, thanks to our wives who have completely supported our "love affair" with this book, and to our parents who have given us the raw material that it takes to achieve our goals.

Prologue

This book found its roots in a number of nagging questions we have asked ourselves about how and why organizations work and don't work. Questions we've wrestled with over the years as we have watched and worked in a myriad of businesses. Eventually we began to see a recurring dilemma that by the mid-1990s had become so prevalent that it cried out for answers. We saw dysfunction, disillusionment, disappointment, distress. We wondered why so much effort was producing so little results? Why, despite grand schemes for advancement, were so many companies not moving forward? Why did highly touted vanguards of change turn into widespread disappointments? Why did the parade of books, articles, and consultants swing from "Here's the cure," to "Here's the antidote for that cure," to "Here's a new cure"?

Tom Peters wrote *In Search of Excellence* in 1988 and began recanting many of his conclusions only a few years later. In 1993 Michael Hammer brought us *Reengineering,* and by 1996 he, too, was well into recantations. For every business news story that sung the battle hymn of successful organizational change, there were hundreds of untold stories of losses, failures, and struggles to survive—even some of the winners of the prestigious Baldrige Awards went in the tank. In the streets, in reality, there were more losers than winners, more coming up short than coming out winning. Of course, all this has led to the next wave of books and articles about what was going so terribly wrong, and why. And we're smack-dab in the middle of that trend, trying to understand why so many have made such little progress. Instead of another rush to change, however, we contend that organizations need to first get at the fundamental footings of how and why they operate the way they do. We need to think before we run our organizations over the precipice like lemmings in pursuit of the miracle program that will at last solve all our problems.

As we began to dig inside our own experiences and thinking, to explore the experiences and thinking of others, and to look back on the road traveled by so many companies, we turned up more questions than answers—along with some very exciting possibilities. But there was one question for which we could not find a satisfactory answer: If most of us, as business practitioners operating business organizations, are ostensibly good at what we do, why has so much of what we've done been so wrong? What were we thinking? It was this last question which opened a pathway for us that we have been pursuing ever since. What have we been thinking?

This led us back to what seems to have been ignored for a long time: the fundamental thinking behind what we do in our organizations, and why we do it. Thinking is what dictates decisions and actions, and if the action is wrong then it stands to reason that the thinking behind the action is wrong, too. But how could the thinking be so off if so many of the decisions we make seem right at the time? Are they all wrong? No, they aren't. Some of the specific ideas and intentions are right, but what is way off is the understanding of the context in which we make decisions and take action. When it comes to context, our thinking has been wrong—dead wrong. The thinking in organizations is rooted in old context because we are unable to understand and cope with the new context of an ever-changing world. So while the world radically changes in time, space, and context, the organization remains much the same. We asked ourselves if current thinking can get us where we need to be in order to survive. Our answer? An unequivocal no. This was the leaping off point for our new thinking, and for this book.

Many organizations are not capable of handling the future, and they cannot significantly change that capability by trying to apply the majority of today's prescribed remedies and fixes. That's because all of these "cures" still reside in the old context. We discovered that there are a number of deeply ingrained assumptions, everyday givens, that have a tremendous impact on the way companies operate. When we looked at these in the light of rampant change, we saw a glaring mismatch. Our old, staunchly held beliefs and assumptions about how to operate companies were way out of whack with the realities of the surrounding world. External, centrifugal change has forced organizations to jump, turn, and twist every which way, but internally—at the core of the organization—nothing of substance has changed. The thinking that drives everything has experienced little or no change. And until some of the fundamental thinking changes, real, sustainable change cannot happen. Until the majority of people in the organization see and understand the dramatically forming context of the new era, they will never be able to respond to it—and they *are* the organization.

We understand that it's next to impossible to change everyone's thinking in anything less than a decade or even a generation. We do believe, however, that you can begin to change thinking by creating a framework or platform for new thinking that is in sync with the ever-changing realities that the organization must deal with everyday. People can then have access to this new thinking, which in turn allows them to determine the basis for their own thinking in view of the overall operating platform of thought. The analogy to software in computers makes sense here: new operating platforms and master programs are installed in order to allow other programs to operate and function effectively. That's why we call our new thinking thoughtware. We must upgrade our organizations' thoughtware before we can operate and function effectively.

Once we realized that we had to change fundamental thinking to make sustainable change a reality, it didn't take us long to identify the key planks in the old platforms of thinking—the old thoughtware. We came up with such issues as costs, quality, productivity, response to customers, structure, bureaucracy, control, empowerment, measurement, capacity, utilization, and so on. We were able to boil most of these down and group them in a few categories and thus found that most of the old thoughtware rested on four planks: division of labor, departmentalization, span of control, and point of authority.

We then set out to look at how the new context of the world around us impacts on these set-in-cement blocks of thinking. This brought us to the point of defining four of the most dominant forces driving the new context. We identified these drivers as: the power of relationships and horizontal process; unlimited access to information; the imperatives of speed, flexibility, and focus; and the fundamental need for a hierarchy of accountability. We looked at these drivers of the new thoughtware up against the planks in the old thoughtware and asked, What has to change? What new thinking needs to be in place in order to let go of the old thoughtware and create an organization that is capable of dealing with these drivers of the new context? From this we established the four most pivotal planks of the new thoughtware platform: knowledge of the whole, measurement of what matters, a focus on time to action, and allowment. This gave us the framework for the new thoughtware, as well as the basis for this book.

Thoughtware is not another new and improved management concept or enabling methodology like TQM or activity-based management. It is not leadership dogma. It is much more fundamental. Thoughtware is like the DNA, the genetic makeup of every organization. Stretching the words of French philosopher René Descartes, who said, "I think, therefore I am," we say, "As the organization thinks, so it will be," or, "Change the thinking and the organization will change itself." It's that systemic. That rooted. Thoughtware is not a program; it's already embedded in every organization, pushing, pulling, forming, and driving operations. The only question is, is it the right thoughtware?

So as not to be branded as another Johnny-come-quick fix and to guard against what might speciously seem like a swallow-the-whole-darn-thing prescription, we offer our thinking as a work in progress. We expect to see it grow, compound, multiply, and give birth to new thoughtware. At this point in time, we believe we have opened the door to the underpinnings of what makes organizations what they are and are not, and if we can encourage organizations to look at their inherent thoughtware and consider something new, then we have fashioned the beginnings of a true breakthrough. In fact, it's already happening: Many organizations are deep in the throes of expelling old thoughtware and installing new, and realizing incredible, never-expected results. We hope this book is a means for expanding that horizon.

PART ONE

context

Think About It   1

I was to learn later in life that we tend to meet any new situation by reorganizing; and a wonderful method it can be for creating an illusion of progress while producing confusion, inefficiency, and demoralization.

—Petronius Arbiter, 66 a.d.

What Does Bill Know?

What was Bill Gates thinking when he allowed the focus, strategy, priorities, and allocation of resources of Microsoft, a multi-billion dollar corporation, to change so dramatically—in just six months? That's some change! And technology wasn't the driver of the change, it was knowledge. Knowledge of what was happening with technology (specifically the Internet). Knowledge of what could happen. Knowledge of what the future could be with the Internet. Obviously, Microsoft is technology based, technology driven, and technology dependent, but it's their thinking about what that technology means, and their thinking about the future, and their built-in capability to change that drove the organization to shift in a nanosecond from a strategy that largely ignored the Internet to one that centered on it.

Gates has done what few executives have dared. He has taken a thriving, $8 billion, 20,000 employee company and done a massive about-face—in six months!

> *I can't think of one corporation that has had this kind of success and, after twenty years, just stopped and decided to reinvent itself from the ground up. What they're doing is decisive, quick, breathtaking.*
> —JEFFREY KATZENBERG, DREAMWORKS SKG

We shouldn't let the mystique of Bill Gates or the high-tech image of Microsoft feed our ever-present, warped assumption that is so often expressed in the familiar refrain, "Yeah, but—they're different from us." This is one of history's oldest statements in defense of the fear of change, and one of our most infamous excuses for staying stuck. What Gates has done must not be looked upon as the exception, it is the rule of the future—be prepared and capable of changing everything in a nanosecond (in business change chronology six months is a nanosecond) or be lost in history. We should look at the commonality in this extraordinary feat of change. What Gates and, more importantly, thousands of employees at Microsoft have done is springboard—catapult is a more appropriate term—into a whole new context. And the foundation for their leap was anchored in new thinking.

Microsoft isn't alone. Other companies' rapid changes may not be as dramatic, but their leaders are making significant changes in structure and direction by applying new thinking to their organizations. Honda, the auto success of the 1980s, began falling apart in the early 1990s. Car sales fell in 1993 and 1994, Honda completely missed the sport utility vehicle boom, and business dried up. Then, in just two years (1994–1996), the company underwent intense internal change and zoomed ahead of competitors to enjoy the greatest success in its 48-year history.

Other examples abound. Starbucks, the booming coffee chain, is a fascinating study of growth through the application of new thinking. From one store in the early 1970s to over 800 today, Starbucks' growth stems from very different, at-odds thinking: Get into a commodity business (coffee), charge more than the competition, and make customers line up for your product. And when the company opens a new site, it offers free coffee for the first 30 days so the employees can practice. New thinking also allowed Nissan to see itself as being in the human transportation business, not the car business. This change led to the development of a roadside assistance program (later adopted by competitors).

Similarly, Whirlpool sees itself in the garment preservation business, not the durable goods, white appliance business. This has led to integration and collaboration with manufacturers of garments and makers of cleaning products. Wal-Mart recognized that it wasn't simply in the retail business, it is in the distribution business. And Nordstrom has become the benchmark for customer service in its retail department stores, where anything in the store can be purchased anywhere in the store, and one salesperson may escort you from department to department to ensure that all your needs are met.

These are but a few examples of where new thinking has changed the rules of competition. The world around us is changing so fast that much of what we did yesterday, what we know today, and what we think works, has nothing to do with tomorrow. The very context in which we live, and in which we must run our companies, has changed so dramatically that much of what we do, know, and think no longer fits, no longer works.

And too often history repeats itself: The economy grows, the economy slows. Unemployment increases, unemployment decreases. Companies flourish, companies flounder. Companies grow, companies downsize. Companies restructure, companies regress. We take two steps forward and two back, and positive, sustainable change remains elusive. We can't seem to achieve sustainable good. We only generate sporadic, temporary gains. And then—you guessed it—history repeats itself.

Old stalwarts like RCA and Pan Am have come face to face with their history. IBM, Kodak, AT&T, Sears, CBS, and many more corporations large and small have found the forces of change too often bring them full circle to nowhere. Even the much revered Motorola had begun to see cracks in its great change machine by 1996. "This year's [1996] setbacks have shattered the aura of invincibility that had been gathering around the company and underscored the increasing challenge it faces in staying nimble enough to pick out and master the most valuable 21st century technologies."[1]

During the decade of the 1980s, a total of 230 companies— 46 percent—disappeared from the Fortune 500.[2]

Of course, most of us are more comfortable with the past than the future. The past is tangible—it's happened, we know it—whereas the future is completely speculative. Therefore, we depend on, lean on, and use the past to chart our future course. Based on the past we know, we develop feasibility studies, elaborate forecasts, and research to decide what to do in the future. Many would say that this approach has served us well:

Look at the growth, the prosperity, the progress, and the prof-its, they say. Others would say it has failed us: Look at the regression, the failures, the layoffs, the unemployment, the environment, the debt, the poverty, and the decline, they argue. Regardless of which viewpoint we hold, we can agree that there is a common and growing sense of futility in trying to fig-ure out the future by looking to the past. It doesn't work any-more, especially in organizing and running our companies.

> *It's a question of whether we're going to go forward*
> *into the future, or past to the back.*
> —Vice President Dan Quayle

At no time in our history has the past been as incapable of providing us with learning-lessons as it is today. And yet we continue to look back to get ahead. The most important lesson learned from hindsight and experience should be that it is becoming more and more irrelevant and inadequate. Think about the following statements:

- Who the hell wants to hear actors talk? (Harry Warner, Warner Bros. Studio, 1927)
- There is no reason why anyone would want to have a computer in their home. (Ken Olson, Digital Equipment Corp. founder, 1977)
- Radio has no future. Heavier than air flying machines are impossible. X-rays will prove to be a hoax. (William Thomson, scientist, 1824–1907)
- Space travel is utter bilge. (Sir Richard Von Der Riet Wooley, *The Astronomer Royal,* 1956)
- While theoretically and technically television may be fea-sible, commercially and financially I consider it an impos-sibility. (Lee DeForest, American inventor, 1873–1961)

- Computers in the future will weigh no more than 1.5 tons. (*Popular Mechanics,* 1949)
- 640k ought to be enough for anybody. (Bill Gates, Microsoft CEO, 1981)

> *You can never plan the future by the past.*
> —EDMUND BURKE, 1791

Forget history. We must look ahead. But just looking (and planning) ahead is not enough. Having vision, goals, strategies, and plans to get to the future will not ensure our getting there. This is because *we can't get to the future from where we are.* We have to start from a different place, a new context.

We often hear people say, "You're taking that out of context," implying that we're drawing a misleading conclusion. But we never hear people say, "You're *doing* that out of context." You can't *do* something out of context. You can think out of context, but you can't *do* out of context. Context is always there, as the surrounding conditions in which we act, and it is created by an aggregation of history, facts, findings, fantasies, events, opinions, assumptions, concepts, thoughts, perceptions, and actions. We live and do and die in context, and today, as never before, we are frighteningly aware that the context in which we live is undergoing radical, disruptive, even violent change—every day. Driven by economics, technology, divergence, disparity, and social dysfunction, the context of the world around us is in turmoil. Disruption is a given, and rampant change a fact of life:

- Between 1960 and 1990, output of manufactured goods of all kinds continued to rise, but the number of jobs required to create that flow of production fell by half.[3]

- Already two-thirds of U.S. employees work in the service sector and knowledge is becoming our most important product.[4]
- In 1960 half the industrialized countries in the world were involved in making things, but by 2000 no industrialized country will have more than one-sixth or one-eighth of its economy based in the traditional role of making and manufacturing.[5]
- In the U.S. the contingent work force consists of approximately 45 million temps, part-time, and self-employed people.[6]
- Corporations spent more than one trillion dollars in the 1980s on computers, robots, and other automated equipment.[7]
- Today's average consumers wear more computer technology on their wrist than existed in the entire world before 1961.[8]
- More information has been produced in the last 30 years than during the previous 5,000.[9]
- A weekday edition of *The New York Times* contains more information than the average person was likely to come across in a lifetime during 17th century England.[10]

These examples are evidence to how drastically the outside context continues to change. Yet within our organizations, where the great majority of us work, the internal context has barely changed at all. Organizational context stands stagnant while the encompassing context in which we have to do business swirls around us like a gale-force-12 storm.

We've made lots of changes in our organizations over the past 10 to 15 years, to be sure. But it's been *content* change, not *context* change. Therein lies a huge problem: Changing the content without changing the context will only take us so far, and that's not very far. In fact, it's not even close to where we have to be.

Stop... and Think

Before we mount yet another charge into the valley of change we need to stop and think. Why has so much change effort produced so few lasting results? In 1994, for example, $32 billion was spent on reengineering and two-thirds of it failed.[11] Similarly, a total quality management survey reported that 73 percent of the 300 companies surveyed had had total quality management (TQM) programs underway for some time, but 63 percent of the companies had failed to improve quality defects by even 10 percent.[12]

Over the years, why have the heralded tools of change—like reengineering, activity-based management, open-book management, economic value added, leadership dogma, and TQM—all fallen short of expectations? We hear many reasons: lack of commitment, lack of empowerment, lack of a companywide coalition, peoples' resistance to change, and so on. But no reason is more compelling, and none offers a greater potential for dramatic change, than the thought that much of what we have attempted has been done *within the wrong context*. We keep changing content without ever changing the context in which we place new content.

Programmatic Addiction

No term better describes the North American love affair with change programs than *addiction*. An addiction is nothing more than a repetitive behavior that leads us to be dishonest with ourselves without knowing it. We define *program addiction* as an *unrecognized pattern of behavior that leads to unproductive or unfulfilling consequences*. Sound familiar? It is to millions of employees who have for years been absorbing program after program after program in pursuit of substantial change, the ultimate organizational satisfaction. The results? Little change and more addiction.

By definition, a program has a beginning and an end. Therein lies the problem. Change has no end. Program addiction is pandemic, and it continues its powerful hold on organizations as it destroys their ability to cope with the future, despite the fact that there is no valid demonstration, and no measure, that people can effectively absorb and integrate programmatic change into everything they handle on a day-to-day basis. Nonetheless, we keep overdosing. And because we are so addicted to the programs, our minds lack objectivity, our thoughts lack clarity, and we never see the contextual limitations in which we are trying to operate. So programs wither and die, and the context goes unchanged. Organizations are mired in misperceptions and misunderstandings, and in spite of burgeoning technology and a flurry of innovation, we still operate from deeply entrenched platforms of old thinking and old context. Until we change that thinking, the degree of change we achieve will be severely restrained.

Productivity Obsession

If programs are an addiction, then our pursuit of greater productivity is an obsession. However, while investment in information technology in the white collar sector has multiplied by 700 percent since 1962, productivity essentially has flatlined during the same period (see Figure 1-1). Yet, in spite of evidence to the contrary, corporations continue to count on technology to improve productivity. Consider that today the power of a personal computer microchip doubles every 18 months while the cost of computing is cut by roughly 30 percent every year. Productivity has increased in certain segments where technology easily replaces human work (e.g., transaction support areas, robotics); however, it has yet to prove much productivity advantage in white collar knowledge jobs.[13] Or anywhere. From 1961 to 1973, the productivity of labor and capital in 18 industrial companies increased by an average of 24 percent a year. From 1974 to 1992 the international average was .9 percent.[14]

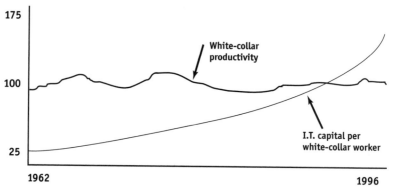

Data source: U.S. Department of Labor Statistics

Figure 1-1. Information Technology Investment Outpaces Productivity

Corporations also have counted on layoffs and downsizing to increase productivity. Mass layoffs, however, are counter-productive. They destroy loyalty, job stability, and continu-ity—the very ingredients of productivity. According to an American Management Association survey, only 45 percent of downsized companies reported any increase in operating prof-its (the main reason for making the cuts in the first place) and 67 percent had had to make a second or even a third round of cuts. The survey also found that the most likely effect of down-sizing was a slump in morale, which can reduce productivity and profits.[15] In short, layoffs have not delivered the productivity improvements promised and the long-term effects are an even bigger question.

Stephen Roach, chief economist and director of Global Economic Analysis at Morgan Stanley, made the following disturbing comments about downsizing in the *Harvard Business Review*:

> Restructuring has a dark side, one that has prompted my second thoughts. Instead of focusing on investment in innovation and human capital—the heavy lifting required to boost long-term productivity—corporate strategies have become more and more focused on downsizing and compressing their costs. The result is increasingly hollow companies that may be unable to maintain, let alone expand, market share in the rapidly growing global economy. If that's all there is to the productivity-led recovery, the nation could well be on a path toward industrial extinction. A major rethinking is in order.[16]

We have chosen short-term programmatic change over long-term growth. Substantive, sustained change that can get us to the future has not happened. Although some of what we have done has been useful, the questions remain: What is really necessary? How much downsizing is of value and how much is destructive? Yes, we must remove "corporate fat," but do we recognize what is fat and what is bone? Do corporate downsizers know the real value of layoffs beyond the short-term share "hit"? As Roach points out,

> Downsizing means making do with less—realizing efficiencies by pruning both labor and capital. Sustained productivity growth, however, hinges on getting more out of more by deriving increased leverage from an economy's (company's) expanding resource base. Downsizing is a recipe for capitulation of market share, as industries increasingly short on capacity lack the wherewithal to meet expanding demand.[17]

First the Necessary, Then the Useful

In the rush to change our organizations, chase markets, and pump share price, we have been blind to the seismic shifting of context. We have done much that is useful, but little that is necessary, by repeatedly playing with layers while ignoring the core; we have demonstrated a *dogmatic adherence to the past* that has oppressively curtailed our ability to get to the future. We must move on, beyond the thinking of that great comic strip philosopher, Pogo, who once said, "The uncertainty of misery is better than the misery of uncertainty." Because in today's world, uncertainty is a given as never before, but it need not be a bedfellow with misery.

We keep trying to improve productivity by increasing the utilization of resources instead of reconfiguring and reallocating the availability of resources. We keep counting and cutting labor costs (which are often not a major driver of costs) instead of getting at the huge overhead burden and waste. We maintain the same old financial measures to track a lot of what doesn't matter while ignoring the measurement of things that really matter, such as the value of intellectual capital. We reengineer with scores of new-fangled techniques while never addressing the very context within which we are attempting to reengineer. We continue to fix the traditional organization instead of creating a whole new one. And so, the parade of the past keeps marching on.

Critical Thinking

He who learns but does not think is lost!
He who thinks but does not learn is in great danger!
—CONFUCIUS

One of the most remarkable thinkers on organizations today is Dr. Elliott Jaques. His work, even more than the reknowned Peter Drucker, has withstood the test of time. A philosopher, scientist, author, and revolutionary thinker, his more than 50 years of study, research, writings (17 books), and applied work have culminated in some undeniable conclusions about the phenomena of work and organization, all strongly supported by scientific findings and empirical evidence. Dr. Jaques has made an enormous contribution to the understanding of organizations, how they operate, and how people function—or don't function—within them. His two most recent books, *Requisite Organization* and *Human Capability,* are cornerstones in a foundation of thinking that forces us to seriously rethink much of what we currently accept. In no uncertain terms, and with rock-solid scientific support, Dr. Jaques' thinking challenges the fundamental precepts of organizational design. Two of his many principles are:[18]

• *Human capability and its role in employee organizations* can *be measured.* To date, behavioral scientists claim human behavior cannot be measured. But Jaque's findings refute this. He also states that it can be integrated within a requisite organization, in accordance with a natural and required hierarchy, to allow for the realization of the full potential of every employee and the optimum managerial system.

• *There must be a fundamental structure of managerial hierarchy with the requisite accountability between a manager, a subordinate, and a manager-once-removed in any employment system.* That's a much different viewpoint than "flatten," "downsize," or "create self-managing teams." When this essential structure of managerial accountability is absent (which it is in most cases) the organization will be highly dysfunctional.

These two principles of Jacque's and their integration into any employment organization are, in fact, core determinants of an organization's capability to perform effectively. This is paramount thinking that cannot be ignored if we are to hold any real hope of changing our organizations for the better.

Another modern-day thinker is Edward de Bono. In one of his many books, *Teach Yourself to Think,* he states, "We have a traditional thinking system which is excellent as far as it goes but inadequate."[19] He goes on to say that we must move beyond the thinking system of the "Gang of Three" [Socrates, Plato, Aristotle], in which "we find our way around by fitting new experiences into the boxes [principles] derived from the past. This is perfectly adequate in a stable world where the future is the same as the past—but totally inadequate in a changing world where old boxes do not apply." De Bono further contends that "such problems will not yield to more analysis.... We need to design a way forward, leaving the cause in place." In other words, we must move into a new context.

Richard Pascale and Tracy Goss, authors and consultants, in writing about reinventing the organization, argue that altering an organization's context is the decisive factor in paving the way for transformation. They suggest that the term *context* encompasses the underlying assumptions or invisible premises on which an organization and its strategies are based.[20] Stanley Davis, in *Future Perfect,* states that the only way for an organization to get to the future is "to lead from a place in time that assumes that you are already there, and that is determined even though it hasn't happened yet."[21]

All of these eminent thinkers offer thoughts that serve as bright shafts of light, probing the depths of organizational morass, trying to enlighten our current thinking and illuminate a way out of our long-set and hardened old context. Do we listen? Do we absorb? Do we question? Do we understand the lack of new thinking in our organizations and the magnitude of our current ignorance? What they are all saying, essentially, is that *if* we want to get to the future, we have to start *in* the future. We must operate as if we are already there, in the future. We have to *be* there, *think* there. We have to create a future context in which we think and operate *today*.

Contextual change can happen only if we are able to change our foundational *thoughtware*. We define thoughtware as *the collective framework of thinking, rooted in the perceptions and assumptions of the organization's membership, that dictates how the members behave and interact.* The organization operates on, and is run by, its thoughtware. The elements of thoughtware functioning in an organization combine to form its internal context and to determine how the organization as a whole performs.

From Old Thoughtware to New Thoughtware

There is a way of getting from old context to new context. As this book sets out, the process begins with a sound understanding of philosophy married to a unique application of techniques. This union requires a reaching out beyond current thinking, by taking into account three key notions: the collective framework of thinking, the driving principles of new context, and the key components of the emerging new thoughtware. As illustrated in Figure 1-2, the old thoughtware consisted of four parts: division of labor, departmentalization, limited span of control, and concentrated (and misplaced) point of authority. The context drivers—the principles that drive the new context in which we operate—are relationships and horizontal process; information flow; speed, flexibility, and focus: and hierarchy of accountability. Finally, the new thoughtware consists of knowledge of the whole, measurement of what matters, a focus on time to action, and allowment. Each of these concepts will be explained and connected in the remainder of the book as we explore how to rebuild the thoughtware of organizations.

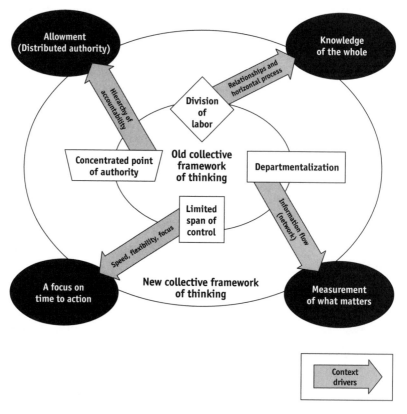

Figure 1-2. A New Collective Framework of Thinking

Notes

1 "Some Humbling Times for a High-Tech Giant," *The New York Times,* October 13, 1996, p. 3-1.

2 Price Pritchett, *New Work Habits for a Radically Changing World* (Dallas: Pritchett & Associates, 1995), p. 49.

3 Jeremy Rifkin, *The End of Work* (New York: G.P. Putnam's Sons, 1995), p. xii.

4 Peter F. Drucker, *Post-Capitalist Society* (from Pritchett, *New Work Habits for a Changing World,* p. 1).

5 Ibid., p. 1

6 Mary O'Hara-Deveraux and Robert Johansen, *Global Work: Bridging Distance, Culture and Time* (from Pritchett, *New Work Habits for a Radically Changing World,* p. 44).

7 Rifkin, *The End of Work,* p. 6.

8 Ian Morrison and Greg Schmidt, *Future Tense: The Business Realities of the Next Ten Years* (from Pritchett, *New Work Habits for a Radically Changing World,* p. 37).

9 Saul Wurman, *Information Anxiety* (from Pritchett, *New Work Habits for a Radically Changing World,* p. 21).

10 Jack Trout, *The New Positioning* (New York: McGraw Hill, 1996).

11 Bruce Caldwell, "Missteps, Miscues," *Information Week,* June 1994, p. 50.

12 Robert Schaffer and Harvey Thompson, "Successful Change Programs Begin with Results," *Harvard Business Review,* January–February 1992, p. 80.

13 "Rethinking Work," *Business Week,* October 17, 1994, p. 80.

14 "Productivity Paradox Puzzles Experts," *The Globe,* April 14, 1997, p. B1.

15 "Upsizing," *The Economist,* February 10, 1996, p. 61.

16 Stephen Roach, "The Hollow Ring of the Productivity Revival," *Harvard Business Review,* November–December 1996, pp. 81–82.

17 Ibid., p. 82.

18 From a David Hughes interview with Elliott Jaques, October 1996.

19 Edward de Bono, *Teach Yourself to Think* (London: Penguin Group, 1995), p. 8.

20 Tracy Goss, Richard Pascale, and Anthony Athos, *Reinventing Strategy and the Organization: Managing the Present from the Future.* Reprinted from *The Portable MBA Strategy,* Fahey and Randall, Ch. 16.

21 Stanley Davis, *Future Perfect* (Reading, MA: Addison-Wesley, 1987), p. 25.

What's Wrong with the Current Context? | 2

> *Faced with the alternative between changing one's mind and proving it unnecessary, just about everybody gets busy on the proof.*
>
> —John Kenneth Galbraith

The current organization context is familiar, real, and understood, so why change it? Because it doesn't fit almost anything that is happening. It's incompatible, out of sync, doomed to failure. And yet we spend most of our time and effort defending the current context—and thereby perpetuating ignorance.

We're stuck in old thinking. Mesmerized with chasing control, seeking stability, and trying to predict the unpredictable when in fact these are the very things that keep us nailed down in old context. The world can't be predicted; it's too chaotic. We shouldn't attempt to predict. Instead, we need to build the capability to respond as fast as possible, without prediction. We must reallocate resources to build fast, flexible systems that are indifferent to unpredictability. We must create a new context, one that thrives on turbulence.

Only New Thinking Can Change Context

To think is first of all to create a world (or to limit one's
own world, which comes to the same thing).

— ALBERT CAMUS

All human behavior is rooted in thought. People's thoughts and assumptions are the basis for all their actions and interactions. Errors of thinking are not errors of logic but of perception. Context is perceived in the mind and defined in the thinking, and in an organization the sum of the people's collective thinking—the organization's thoughtware—is the prime determinant of the organization's internal context and the leverage to its capability and performance.

context *n. the interrelated conditions in which something*
exists or occurs; parts that surround [a thing or event] . . .
and can throw light on its meaning.

How we perceive context can be somewhat different, or a whole lot different, than the reality. Our perception is totally dependent on *what we know* of the world, and *what we think* of whatever is currently confronting us. The context in which we perceive ourselves working usually matches our pattern of experience and thought, and how we perceive context dictates what we do and why we do it. If that perception badly contorts the reality, then no matter what we do the outcome will never work in reality. In our hell-bent-for-leather stampede to find change solutions, we continually charge over the hill without questioning or understanding the context in which we're trying to make change happen, and the perceived context is way out of line with reality. So we just keep firing more content within the same old context—and not much changes.

The heart of the problem comes from not understanding the critical importance of context and not wanting—that's right, not wanting—to change our perception of the context. For most people it is easier, more comfortable, less threatening to stay in the current context, rather than face the risk of *what might be* in a new context. So current perception stays put and its collective power within the organization ignores new context, thereby limiting the organization to a cursed existence in old context. And the old internal context is so out of whack with the realities of the new external context that the organization remains ineptly dysfunctional. Our organizations are like fish out of water: the context has changed but they're still trying to swim as if in the stream, when in reality they're just flipping and flopping to nowhere.

Contextual change can only happen *if we are able to change our foundational thinking,* and it begins with perception. Edward de Bono talks about the limits of perception in his book, *Serious Creativity,* and how we do an excellent job at processing information (ie., mathematics, computers), but have done little in developing our perception. He tells a marvelous story of a five-year-old boy in Australia who is offered a choice, by his friends, of selecting and keeping either a $1 coin or a smaller $2 coin.[1] We have recreated the theme of the story here in a dialogue that might take place in any American home.

• It's All in How You Look at It •

Dylan is five years old. Typically, he's in constant pursuit of his nine-year-old brother Chad. And Chad, like most older brothers, is always picking on Dylan. Chad and two of his buddies are hanging out in his room one day when Dylan comes wandering in.

Chad says to his buddies, "Hey guys, wanna get a laugh? Watch this." His friends eagerly gather around. "Dylan, come here."

Dylan, pleased with the invitation, breaks into a big grin and looks up with great anticipation. Chad sits down on the edge of the bed and holds out his hands, palms up. In his right hand is a dime and in his left a nickel. He glances back at his buddies and whispers, "Watch how stupid Dylan is." Turning, he flashes a know-it-all grin at his brother's innocent face. "Hey Dylan, which one of these coins do you want, the big one or the small one?"

Dylan's eyes ponder his choices for just a moment. "This one!" The little guy shoots out his hand, grabs the nickel, jams it in his pocket, and leaves the room.

Chad triumphantly closes his hand on the dime, breaks into a smug smile, and turns for approval from his buddies. Both boys are in stitches. Chad stops chuckling long enough to say, "Is that stupid or what? And he does it every time. I can't believe it—he always falls for it."

"He's so stupid," chimes in one of the buddies.

A large shadow fills the doorway. The laughter is cut short. It's Chad's and Dylan's father. "Chad, your brother is not stupid, and I don't want you playing that trick on him again. Do you hear me?"

He gets a guilty reply. "Yeah, okay. We're just playing, Dad. Dylan doesn't care. He likes it."

His father interjects sternly, "Well, I'll have no more of it, and I'll speak to Dylan, too." He turns and heads for Dylan's room.

"Hi Dylan. How're you doing?"

"Hi Dad." Dylan, sitting in the middle of his bedroom floor surrounded by Lego blocks, hardly looks up.

"Dylan, I want to explain something to you." Lowering himself onto the floor, he leans back against the end of the bed.

"Okay Dad."

The father then spends the next five minutes putting the value of nickels and dimes into context for his son. Using pennies, nickels, dimes, and quarters, he shows his son that the size of the coin does not always represent the value of the coin. Throughout the chat, Dylan listens carefully and his continual head nodding seems to indicate that he understands.

"So, do you see the difference between a nickel and a dime?" asks his father.

"Yeah. A nickel is 5 pennies and a dime is 10 pennies," he answers proudly.

"Good. So the next time Chad asks you to pick a coin, which one are you going to pick?"

"The nickel," came the quick reply.

"No Dylan. Not the nickel, the dime—it's worth twice as much." Exasperation is all over the father's face.

Dylan reaches under his bed and pulls out an old sock. He takes a handful of nickels out of the sock and holds them up to his father. "Yeah, but if I take the dime Chad will stop playing the game with me … and look how many nickels I've gotten from him!"

> *It's very difficult to see things in a different context.*
> —A LEARNED PHILOSOPHER (DYLAN'S FATHER)

By changing context, companies have changed their futures. FedEx changed the very essence of the delivery business. CNN changed the context of broadcast news. And both of these changes began with new thinking. Change the thinking and the context will change. It's that simple. New thinking is the predecessor to changing context and creating sustainable change in our outdated, outmoded organizations. This change requires *new thoughtware* that will allow us to transform new information, create new movement, engage conflict, shift context, and build an organization that can handle the future and all its uncertainty.

We're Only Scratching the Surface

Many of our assumptions, beliefs, perceptions, and methods, all of which create context, are deeply ingrained in our organizations. It takes more than programs and tools to change them, and in the haste to forge tools we too often create commercially packaged, freeze-dried concepts that totally ignore the underlying context. Most of these concepts can be categorized into four basic areas:

- Restructuring (e.g., reengineering, teams, workouts).
- Cost cutting (e.g., downsizing, rightsizing).
- Quality and customer satisfaction (e.g., Quality Circles, TQM, customer focus).
- Value-based dogma (e.g., leadership, empowerment).

Thousands of programs are introduced under these banners and millions of people are affected by them, but they do nothing more than scratch the surface of the context in which they operate. Sooner or later they move from being somewhat useful to being downright detrimental. Their use is usually limited to short-term cost hacking or corporate pep rallies and image making rather than true long-term gain. Because none are based on an intrinsic integration of philosophy and techniques.

Reengineering was this decade's supernova of concepts. But after a three to four year run as the corporate world's hottest management tool (technique), it has exposed its lack of concrete philosophy for growing and sustaining business. In most cases the $4.7 billion reegineering industry has been nothing more than a downsizing exercise. In a *Wall Street Journal* article about Michael Hammer, the so-called guru of reengineering, Hammer himself points out a flaw in his earlier thinking: "I wasn't smart enough about [people]," Hammer says. "I was reflecting my engineering background and was insufficiently appreciative of the human dimension. I've learned that it's critical."[2]

The same article goes on to say that the appeal of the reengineering fad has waned. A survey by Bain & Co. (1996) asked executives at 1,000 companies to rate various management tools. Reengineering didn't score above average in any of five major categories; as a point of comparison, in 1994 it led four of the five categories.[3]

Reengineering is a typical example of a concept with tons of technique and only an ounce of philosophy. As reengineering identified bottlenecks and reconfigured processes to better align resources, it fundamentally ignored the "excess" resources (i.e., the people, the human capital), casting them as unnecessary costs. Look at the upcoming series of figures. The dotted lines in Figure 2-1 represent the maximum throughput attainable at the start of reengineering. In Figure 2-2, the shaded areas outside the maximum throughput channel are the non-value-added activities. In most reengineering cases these resources were dumped—downsized to cut cost and gain efficiency. The result was a leaner organization (Figure 2-3), but with fewer resources and little to no capacity for long-term expansion. It was based on the obsession for short-term productivity gains. The philosophy was *more with less,* but actually it resulted primarily in cost reductions, not increased capacity—

in other words, the same with less. The alternative depicted in Figure 2-4 is based on a different philosophy, one which takes into account the value of *all* resources (especially people) and redeploys those resources to the bottlenecks to expand the potential. This is a philosophy of *more with the same.*

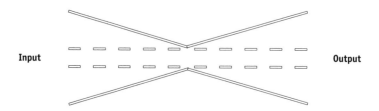

Input   Output

Figure 2-1. The Intent of Reengineering

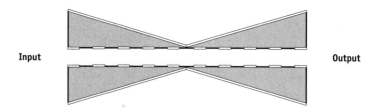

Input   Output

Figure 2-2. Analysis of Reengineering

Input   Output

Figure 2-3. The Result of Reengineering

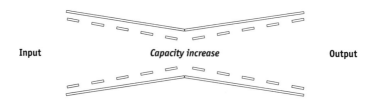

Input   *Capacity increase*   Output

Figure 2-4. What Didn't Happen with Reengineering

Unfortunately, "short-term America" is still driving the bus. Economist Stephen Roach says, "If U.S. companies remain fixated on downsizing, opportunities for growth will vanish before their eyes."[4]

Frighteningly, however, there seems to be no abatement in this trend. In the single month of January 1994, America's largest employers laid off more than 100,000 workers,[5] and in the first five months of 1996 at least 250,000 cuts were announced by big American firms, half as many again as in the same period of the last year.[6] In a 1995 survey of 2,000 corporate executives from the world's leading industrial nations, more than 66 percent of the business leaders predicted that the pace of downsizing and reengineering would increase in the years ahead. The companies surveyed employ 18 million people, more than 6 percent of the work force in the six leading industrial countries.[7] But, despite sharply falling unit-labor costs, fewer than half the firms that have downsized in America during the 1990s have improved profits or productivity.[8] We must move beyond downsizing and its myopic limitations and rebuild our organizations from a different platform.

The Old—and Still Prevalent—Thoughtware Model

Old context is familiar, certain, non-threatening, and understood. That's why it is difficult to change. The tenets of the old context are the givens, the obvious, and the principles with which most of us operate. In fact, the principles are so obvious that we take them for granted and allow them to go unchanged. Our modus operandi is anchored in these contextual pillars.

The great majority of our organizational thinking can be traced to four underlying principles that form much of the context in which our current organizations operate. These principles can be observed in most organizations (see Figure 2-5):

- Division of labor
- Departmentalization
- Limited span of control
- Concentrated point of authority

If we can first understand these bastions of organization and structure, we can then begin to find ways to eradicate them and make way for new thoughtware.

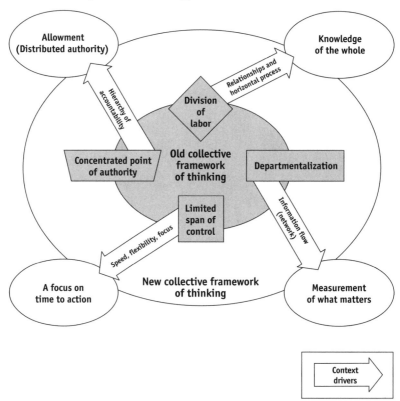

Figure 2-5. An Old Collective Framework of Thinking

Division of Labor

Companies hire, train, and organize employees according to their skills, functions, and responsibilities. The idea has been that specialization delivers economic advantage. Drivers drive; welders weld; supervisors supervise; bellhops hop; maids clean; reservation clerks reserve; waiters wait; wine stewards pour; accountants count; receptionists receive; and presidents preside. All without an overlap. However, dividing up labor according to specialty to gain efficiencies is a practice that doesn't work anymore. It places people in boxes, describes a "job," and stipulates what you are *not* to do. And it leads to compensation systems that are pure alchemy. It's archaic.

Knowledge is transcending this old thoughtware, defying boundaries, and giving people the opportunity to move in many directions as the need requires. Today the most important job to be done is the one not yet being done, but the division of labor creates a labyrinth of barriers that blocks such forward thinking and movement.

• NOT MY JOB •

As the courtesy van pulled up to the Old Context Hotel, I was greeted by a very pleasant doorman. The van driver unloaded several bags from the rear of the van and the doorman placed them on a dolly. The van driver jumped back in the van and announced, "Charley, see you later. I gotta get the van washed."

I wandered into the lobby, followed a minute or two later by the doorman wheeling the dolly just inside the doors. As I waited in one of two lines at the front desk I took in my surroundings. Beautiful hotel, expensive decor, stunning atrium, and a well-dressed, smiling staff. The doorman stood on guard outside, anticipating the next arrivals. Two bellhops waited patiently by their station for the next checked-in guests. An efficient, elegant-looking concierge busied herself behind a great oak desk on the far side of the lobby, and two front desk people scrambled to check in seven new arrivals. At the far end of the front counter was an official-looking woman toiling over some accounting records with another clerk. During the next three or four minutes a very urbane man walked in and out of the back office several times to survey the scene, just to disappear again from whence he came. He must be the resident manager, I thought.

Another couple of minutes passed and I had time to do a quick inventory. One doorman, two bellhops, one concierge, two receptionists, one accountant, one clerk, and a manager. Nine hardworking, well-meaning, trying-to-be-pleasant people, plus seven guests and me. More of them than us. Better than a one-to-one ratio. And yet, more than 10 minutes had passed since I walked through their front door. I slipped off the end of the line and approached the lady deeply focused on her accounting problem.

"Excuse me, I'm in a bit of a rush, do you think someone else could check me in?"

Startled would be an understatement. "Uh ... oh ...." A handful of paper slipped from her hand onto the floor. The clerk scurried to pick them up while the older woman flustered. "I ... I can't check you in sir ... I'm sorry ... you see, I'm in accounting and just happen to be out here checking some records." The younger clerk was frozen, wads of paper clenched in her hands.

I looked surprised. "So, you check out records, but you don't check in guests?" She seemed to be somewhere between apology and anger when the manager spotted the troubling scene and swooped down on us. "May I help you sir?" he asked. The words were right, but the attitude was so wrong. It was obvious he felt I was creating a problem, one serious enough to require his immediate attention, not simply a scanning survey from afar.

"Thank you. I'm in a hurry and wondered if someone else could check me in." You would have thought I'd asked to move the Grand Canyon.

"I'm sorry for the inconvenience sir," he said, but I'm sure he thought *I* was the inconvenience. How dare I suggest disrupting his system by getting accounting people involved in front-desk jobs. How absurd! "We've been hit by a bit of a rush, unexpected arrivals, I'm sure it will just be another moment." He delivered an I-trust-that-will-appease-you smile.

I looked into his beady eyes. "Can *you* check me in?" I could tell I'd asked for another Grand Canyon move.

"Well sir, what I *can* do is take your name and have one of the front-desk personnel check you in when we're not as busy. And I'll have the bellhop check your bags and you can pick them up later." He smiled with such self-satisfaction you'd have thought he had indeed single-handedly moved the Grand Canyon.

I decided to counter. "Perhaps there's someone else who can check me in *now*?"

I couldn't tell whether it was shock or impatience on his face. "I'm sorry sir. That's impossible. You see, everyone has their special duties for which they are trained and there is no one else who knows the check-in procedures and reservations computers." He was frustrated. "Please sir, I assure you we will check you in as soon as we can."

I glanced to my right. All but one of the waiting guests had been checked in. "Thanks anyway. I'll just go through your regular procedures so I don't create too much disruption." He looked relieved as I moved the Grand Canyon back into the proper line.

Two minutes later I was checked in. By then, however, there was no bellhop available, although the concierge, doorman, accountant, clerk, and manager looked all readily available. I decided not to battle again. What chance did I have against the importance of policies, procedures, and accepted practices? I was up against a heavy organizational structure.

I waited. Five minutes later I was in my room. Twenty-five minutes later my bags were delivered.

As shown in Figure 2-6, a customer has one perspective of the flow and events involved in checking into a hotel. Starting with a telephone call to reception (A) requesting a pick up from the airport, the request goes to the doorman, then to the

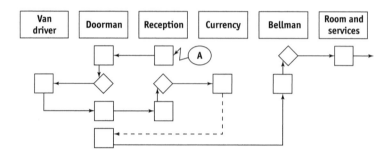

Figure 2-6. Checking into a Hotel: The Customer's Perspective

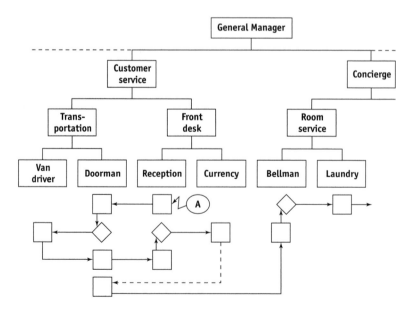

Figure 2-7. Checking into a Hotel: The Hotel's Perspective

van driver who picks up the customer. At the hotel the customer is greeted by the doorman, then the front desk, then handed-off to the cashier for cashing traveler's checks, then back to the doorman for bags, then to the bellman, and to laundry service after all that. The hotel's perspective of the events is very different (Figure 2-7). It's the same series of processes, but they are divided into functions, departments, and disconnected accountabilities because of division-of-labor thinking.

Of course not all hotels operate this way. For example, you will find new thinking at Delta Hotels that declares, "We will check you in in one minute or your room is free." They also offer room service in a specified time or it's free, too. Delta Hotels doesn't operate on division of labor thoughtware. They operate on customer focus and run on new thoughtware that has people move to the task where they are *needed*.

Departmentalization

The power of departments is legendary in American organizations. Not since the Civil War have we known such internal battles. Empires have been built on departmental dominance. Remember when the route to becoming CEO came from the manufacturing floor? Later it was through finance, and then through marketing. The route to success depended on which department was the most important at the time. Everything from careers to the size of VP offices is determined by departmental importance.

Departments are a manifestation of division-of-labor thinking and the grouping of like-thinking—the opposite of *process thinking,* which groups unlike-thinking. Departments are a formidable barrier to meaningful measurement and motivation because they force measurement of the pieces and departmental scoring, thus generating great efficiencies at subsidiary levels instead of across the whole, in an unified direction. Departments are the epitome of divide and rule.

> *The golden rule of departments: Those who have*
> *the most powerful department rule.*

Departmentalization is a destructive force in most organizations, and still, despite all the effort put into teams and cross-functionality, the departmental mind-set is an indelible part of the old context, especially at senior levels.

Limited Span of Control

The struggle and debate continues about how to deal with an organization's traditional span of control: the bureaucracy from whence we run operations. Flatten it? Downsize it? Reengineer it? Keep it? Lose it?

First and foremost, it's obvious that people, not structures and systems, run organizations, and that span of control causes structure. But for what? Ironically, no matter how much we fiddle with structure we don't get at the problem of control. Control has been a doctrine of organizational thinking since the first boss emerged. Ever since, bureaucracy has grown to provide span of control. It looks indomitable, with layers and layers of bosses, piles and piles of reports, stacks and stacks of approvals, and miles and miles of systems, all meant to give us control. In reality, there is very little control. It's an illusion even Houdini could not have created.

The hierarchies have achieved the opposite of what they were intended to achieve. Originally there for the purpose of moving information and maintaining accountability, they have become giant, bureaucratic silos. Except now, technology has changed the context: it has obliterated the need for hierarchy in the movement of information, and the need for quick response has made span of control an impediment. The *only* real purpose of hierarchy is to facilitate accountability (as clearly defined by Elliott Jaques in *Requisite Organization*).

North American companies are the kings of hierarchy. At one time General Motors had 19 levels of management and IBM had 12. However, neither of these companies had control over their destiny. They were not only mired in old thoughtware, they propagated it. Take a look at 10 guiding principles that drove all planning at General Motors from 1970 until the late 1980s:[9]

1. GM is in the business of making money, not cars.
2. Success comes not from technological leadership but from having the resources to quickly adopt innovations successfully introduced by others.
3. Cars are primarily status symbols. Styling is therefore more important than quality to buyers who are, after all, going to trade up every other year.
4. The U.S. car market is isolated from the rest of the world. Foreign competitors will never gain more than 15 percent of the domestic market.
5. Energy will always be cheap and abundant.
6. Workers do not have an important impact on productivity or product quality.
7. The consumer movement does not represent the consensus of a significant portion of the U.S. population.
8. The government is the enemy. It must be fought tooth and nail every inch of the way.
9. Strict centralized financial controls are the secret of good administration.
10. Managers should be developed from within.

This is head-in-the-sand thinking that's difficult to imagine, but it has driven many giant corporations for years. At IBM, CEO John Akers was so removed from the front lines that the prediction that the personal computer business would surpass the mainframe business never got to him the way it should have. Before it got to him the information was either too watered down or ignored, and a huge opportunity was lost—not to mention billions of dollars and untold costs in later layoffs. IBM's subsequent decline is legendary.

The railroads are another good example. Early industrial pioneers of bureaucracy in America, they created spans of control and operating procedures to ensure the safe operation of trains.[10] Today, span of control in the railroad industry has been extended so far that these much-admired captains of industry are out of touch and steering courses to who-knows-where? And all too often, whether in the railroad business or others, the employees are just along for the ride. Span of control has come back to haunt the organization, and in time will destroy it.

Concentrated Point of Authority

Authority (which is not the same as accountability) parallels hierarchy and in the past has created a chain of command that pushes decision making up the organization, further and further from the problem. It compounds the paradox of control. "Get an approval" pushes authority in the wrong direction. "Get a sign off" means the point of authority is in the wrong place. "Issue a change order" means delaying a decision. At Federal Express, the front-line person who deals with the customer has the authority, means, and skills to solve the customer's problems *on the spot*. This is evidence that FedEx knows the point of authority must be at the point of the problem.

But FedEx is the exception, not the rule. In most organizational thinking the old context still rules: Someone with higher authority (supposedly with better information and better skills) must make the decision. It's stifling. Too many organizations are replete with authority in the wrong places, and deplete of accountability as a result.

• SORRY, YOU'RE THE CUSTOMER, WE CAN'T DO THAT •

I had been traveling extensively lately so my home bills were stacked up like Chicago's O'Hare airport on a Friday afternoon. As I flipped through the bills I saw an urgent notice from my insurance broker that required payment within the next few days or the policy would be canceled. I phoned Dewy, Wannabee, Bothered, Inc., my insurance company. After being referred to two "wrong departments" and bounced back to a bewildered receptionist, I finally got a customer service representative.

She was very pleasant. "How may I help you sir?"

"I've been out of town for a couple of weeks and have just now seen your notice of cancellation on a policy I definitely do not want to lapse. How can I ensure it stays in place?"

She asked for the policy number, name, and so on, and then put me on hold for about two minutes. My only companion was the local radio station blaring piped-in music into the telephone system.

"Sorry to keep you waiting sir. Her voice was such a relief—I'd been listening to the Rolling Stones "Can't Get No Satisfaction." "If you send us a check *today* for the full amount of the premium for the next year, we'll be able to keep your policy in force."

"Oh ... uh, today? The full amount?"

"Yes sir. That's correct."

"Well, what I'd *like* to do is put this policy on a series of payments instead of one annual payment." I quickly calculated it would run about $450 a month. "Can I arrange that now, so I don't have to send a check for the full annual premium?"

"Oh, I wouldn't know anything about that sir. But I'm sure we can't make a change like that, especially at this late date." She clearly considered the *late* date as my problem.

With polite impatience, I pushed on. "Could you check for me?"

Hesitation. "Well, like I said, I don't know about these things. I could try to find someone else who might be able to look into such a request and get back to you, but…"

I was going out of town again that night so I was now more than impatient. "Ma'am, I need to speak with someone *now,* please." As I went back on hold I thought how appropriate it would be if the Stones were still chanting "Can't Get No Satisfaction." They weren't. Instead, "Run Around" by Del Shannon came on the air.

Then, "Good morning sir. How may I help you?" It was a very official sounding man.

I went through my request again and was told that he'd have to check with his boss. More wait. More music. This time the local station was playing "It's Just a Matter of Time," by Brook Benton.

"Sorry sir, we can't do that. You see, your policy was originally set up in the computer system as an annual premium account, and a change will require a special requisition and issuance of a new transition policy form, which we would have to send to you for signature. And we will need your authorization in order to set the policy up in our standard, automatic debit system. That will require signatures and an approval from the head office. This might take a couple of weeks."

I thought I'd try one more time. "I can't wait that long. Doesn't anyone there know how to do this, or have the authority to make the change? The policy lapses in a few days and I'm going out of town again. I need to resolve this now."

"Sir, I understand."

I thought, No you *don't,* you don't understand at all. All you understand is what you *can't* do, because the system, company policy, lack of authority, or lack of knowledge, won't let you.

I went for broke. "Let me speak to the president."

"Uh, let me see if he's in sir."

On hold. More music. I smiled as the Beatles' rhythmic lyrics hit me: "Help! I need somebody..."

"Sorry sir, he's out right now, but I could get our vice-president to call you back."

"No thanks. Don't call me, I'll call you." I'd had enough of their pass-it-up-the-line service. "Good-bye." As I hung up, I hoped he would hear the piped-in music. Maybe they'd be playing "Hit the Road, Jack."

I called a friend, got the name of his insurance broker, and phoned. The first representative I spoke to listened to my dilemma.

"No problem sir. I can handle that right now. He took all the relevant information, typed it into his computer while I waited, called someone at my now-former insurance company, and in less than 10 minutes I was on an equal-billing plan with my new insurance company. Hanging up, I began to sing the old James Brown tune, "I feel good... dah, dah, dah, dah, dah, dah... like I knew that I would..."

These four sunk-in-concrete, contextual pylons—division of labor, departmentalization, span of control, point of authority—are the bulwarks against change. They are the deep-seated roots, the creeping ivy of old thoughtware, and they entangle any possible movement toward the future. They are well designed and well ensconced. They bend but they don't break. They are the toll gates on the highway to the future, and we pay the price, every day. To move from the encumbering, restraining context created by such old thoughtware we must first understand some of the main principles that create new context. We'll do just that in the next chapter.

Notes

[1] Edward de Bono, *Serious Creativity* (New York: Harper Business, 1992).

[2] "Management Guru Reengineers Message," *The Wall Street Journal,* November 26, 1996, p. B-11.

[3] Ibid.

[4] Stephen Roach, "The Hollow Ring of the Productivity Revival," *Harvard Business Review*, November–December 1996, p. 89.

[5] Jeremy Rifkin, *The End of Work* (New York: G.P. Putnam's Sons, 1995), p. xvi.

[6] Downsizing and Now Upsizing, *The Economist,* June 8, 1996, p.72.

[7] Jeremy Rifkin, *The End of Work* (New York: G.P. Putnam's Sons, 1995, p. xvi.

[8] "Downsizing and Now Upsizing," *The Economist,* June 8, 1996, p. 72.

[9] James O'Toole, *The Human Resources Planning Journal,* Vol. 10, No. 4, December 1987, p. 254.

[10] Michael Hammer and James Champy, *Reengineering the Corporation* (New York: Harper Business, 1993), p. 13.

Change the Thinking and You'll Change the Context

Things do not change; we change.

—THOREAU

If the old context is so obvious, why is it so hard to change? Because it means changing the very fabric of our thinking in order to break out of old context. Why does the thinking not change? Because minds and organizations have operated for decades within a well-defined context. Our organizational thinking is framed by the contextual givens we discussed in the previous chapter: division of labor, departmentalization, limited spans of control, and concentrated points of authority, as well as structure, layers, chain of command, who's the boss, report to, group decision making, self-managing teams, and linear decision making. In the end, when we are limited by such givens, it doesn't matter how many new ideas and programs we implement; they all are constrained by the overall context within which they have to work. In the compounding rush to rebuild companies, we have designed, created, bought, sold, and implemented a continuous litany of strategies, concepts, and programs—but all of them are merely new content inserted into old context. They have not generated a magnitude of change.

Not Everything Is Wrong

The journey to discovering new organizations and developing new thoughtware does not need to be laden with skeletons of the past. We do not have to throw out everything and start again, nor do we need to yank what we have from its very foundations. In fact, a lot of what we have is okay: We've done a good job with quality. Reengineering, though it did not lead to increased capacity, did help us to discover the transcendence of horizontal processes. We're beginning to corral the proliferation of technology and better manage information. We're getting better at customer focus. And perhaps we'll soon begin to do more than talk about the value of human capital by treating it as an investment, not an expense. All is not wasted.

But Much of It Is

On the other hand, programs such as downsizing have taken a disastrous toll, removing fat, bone, body, and soul from our organizations. Downsizing has enormous negative consequences for the future because it focuses on past and present, *not* on the future. In the new context, short-term profits and share price increases can be anti-future. One of the most important things that true future thinking considers is human capital (the potential value inherent in people), and it builds on continuity and transition planning that invests and transforms this value into productive new assets. Mike Useem, a professor at the University of Pennsylvania's Wharton School of Business, has argued that companies who used downsizing as a corporate strategy were very confused. In reality, rapid flattening of corporate structures created by severe job cuts destroyed morale, damaged customer relationships, and undermined core competencies.

Downsizing is perhaps the most powerful evidence supporting the impeachment of old thinking. People are the only asset that can give us the thinking required to survive in the future; money, technology, and information can't do it. Consequently, the addictive use of this program—to cut loose our human capital—has left a legacy that we will not carry easily into the future. Too many pink slips in the short term may well lead to too much red ink in the long term.

The Lips Are Flapping But the Feet Are Stuck

Too many fly-by-night concepts get by on a truckload of techniques and bafflegab but are void of a well-grounded, deep-thought philosophy. Nowhere is this more serious than in the lack of understanding of our most valued asset, *people.* There's lots of talk but not much walk about how important people are. Read the brochures and listen to the talking heads and you'd think people were indeed valued as the most important asset, but read the unemployment rolls and you know it's a lie.

Unfortunately, the lips keep flapping while the feet are stuck in old thoughtware—thoughtware that says get more with less, cut labor costs, downsize—instead of ascribing to new thoughtware, which says get more with more. It's a fundamental, major difference, and the point of entry in understanding the real value of human capital. Of all the mistakes we've made and all the fundamentals we've ignored, none—*none*—has been more myopic, more void, more damaging, than our thinking on human capital. This time around we must understand it. We must undertake a major rethink.

We have been very good at managing tangible assets and very lousy at managing intangible assets. We've been good with finance and bad with people. Why? We tend to deal with what is tangible, touchable, easy to measure, easy to understand—like history, the past; conversely, we avoid dealing with the intangible, invisible, the difficult to measure, and the difficult to understand—like the future (see Table 3-1). So, we don't give it much thought. More accurately, we give it too much old thought.

Table 3-1. Tangible Versus Human Assets

Tangible Capital (Assets) (Required for business operations)	Human Capital (Assets) (Competitive advantage in knowledge era)
• Readily visible • Rigorously quantified • Part of the balance sheet • Investment produces known return • Can be easily duplicated • Depreciates with use • Has finite application • Managed with "scarcity" mentality • Best leveraged through control • Can be accumulated and stored	• Invisible • Difficult to quantify • Not tracked through accounting • Assessment based on assumptions • Cannot be bought or imitated • Appreciates with purposeful use • Multi-applications without reducing value • Managed with "abundance" mentality • Best leveraged through alignment • Dynamic: short self-life when not used

When our resources can't get us to our aspirations, what do we do? We downsize our aspirations. Why? Because we think we have to have a fit between our resources and aspirations. But we don't. A misfit is good. Powerful. What we need to do is apply new thoughtware that says hold the aspirations and leverage the resources. Specifically, leverage the resource most capable of achieving the aspirations: human capital. Because human capital is not a finite asset. More gets you more, *if* you understand it, think about it, and see it differently.

Human capital in the knowledge era is a rare and exceptional resource and to disregard it is pure folly. Hoard it, build it, leverage it, invest in it. As Paul Zane Pilzer states in his book, *Unlimited Wealth,* to survive in the new economy we must recognize that the return we get from our supply of labor is entirely dependent on how much we are willing to invest in it.

This is the exact opposite of the old thinking in the old economy, which views labor as an inescapable cost of doing business and where the trick is to get the most out of the best, and fewest, workers for the lowest cost.[1] This way of thinking is where corporate downsizers like Al "Chainsaw" Dunlap, CEO of Sunbeam, come from. This is the old school, short-term America. There's no question that Dunlap makes a huge impact on stock values (lining his pockets with obscene amounts of money on his way through), but only time will tell what the long-term results will be. Has he thrown the baby out with the bathwater? Should the corporation look beyond immediate shareholder return? And who are the share-holders? Are they not, in fact, many of the employees who have millions invested through pension funds and mutual funds in the very companies Dunlap and his colleagues are viciously downsizing? They truly don't understand. Worse, they don't value or care about human resources.

When it comes to human capital, there have been times when intentions to get the most value out of people were good, but the attempts have been abysmal. We have totally misunderstood the issue of human capital, its value, and its leverage potential. We have tried to measure its value by using traditional measuring methods—screening devices like discounted cash flows that cannot measure the real value of human capital. The thinking has been, and still is, dead wrong as we dump more and more people onto the unemployment rolls. We must stop and think. Think long term. Think sustained growth. Think about the knowledge era. Think about where knowledge lies. How knowledge grows. How knowledge gets transformed into something of value. Obviously, it begins with human capital.

Moving forward requires that we build with human capital, and that requires new thinking. We've all heard the catchy saying, "If it ain't broke, break it"? Well, it's the organizational thinking that must break. Only when we change the thinking will we learn how to change the organization. It's that simple and that difficult. But it's doable.

• OLD HABITS DIE HARD •

There once was a company named Words, Inc., which manufactured words for every occasion. Words, Inc., had become a market leader in a ferociously competitive market by building on its strengths, especially its ability to develop product line extensions by manufacturing new words from current words. Words, Inc., continually expanded product lines from single letters and maximized the expansion of each. From *A* came *AT* and then *RAT,* and from *I* came *IN* and *IF* and *IS.* Because of the product design and the multiple production lines, the company was able to get long runs with quick changeovers, have high utilization, and achieve significant economies of scale. Words, Inc., had designed its entire operation—from raw material sourcing to customer service—around this successful expansion strategy.

One day, however, Words, Inc., realized that its competitors were doing the same thing and product parity was setting in. The top brass held many meetings to try to determine what to do. Most of the managers believed in their strategy and products, and recommended striving for even greater efficiencies through higher utilization, expanded capacity, and lower prices. Many didn't want to give up on their tried and true products like *RAT* and *AT*.

So the company began to compete on price. They geared up to increase volume and improve the productivity of every product line. For example, they added two more product extensions to the *A* line:

Original product	*A*
New content	*AT*
Add more content	*RAT*
Continue to expand content	*RATE*
Continue to expand content	*GRATE*

A few months later the news was not good. The manufacturing department proudly announced the fill rate was up to 92 percent and they were pushing the limit of their capacity. The engineering department introduced a new *D* to expand the current *GRATE* product to *GRATED*. But the marketing department said they needed new and different products for their customers who were expecting more choices and more customization. The finance department then reported that even though unit sales were up slightly, revenue was off and margins had eroded terribly. The company was also carrying too much finished goods inventory. It was a dilemma.

The breakthrough came from a recently formed cross-functional project team. They had started out as a self-managed team, but soon the team leader, who saw the products of Words, Inc. in a different light, realized that no one was willing to be accountable for the consequences of their new ideas, so he took on the accountability and confirmed it with the president. He didn't think of *GRATE* as an expansion of *RATE*. Instead, he looked for a whole new product. He got the team to step back and think outside their traditional context, which was based on the deeply imbedded way they were used to running the business. He emphasized how time-to-market and response time in meeting custom orders was far more critical than many of the traditional costs they kept trying to reduce.

He had a tough time, however. One of the team members was the original designer of *RAT,* and he wasn't about to dismantle his baby or rush it through engineering. "Besides," he said, "it couldn't be done." And because it was a standard product, the manufacturing people insisted on building buffer inventory.

But because a senior-level, cross-functional team had dissolved departmental barriers and set this team up as a process-complete team, with the team leader accountable for results, soon they were all working outside the normal boundaries. Then, when provoked to think Why not? they began to shift the context. To accommodate the trepidation of the *RAT* engineer they first simulated numerous possibilities. The result was *GREAT.* They had thought through how to reconfigure and create a new product without employing any new assets, and they discovered it could be assembled quickly. It was a first breakthrough. They realized that by applying new thinking and changing the context, they could open up exciting new opportunities. They went into production.

GRATE became	*GREAT*
Again, they changed the thinking using fewer assets	*TREAT*
Then, they changed the thinking again and added more content	*TARGET*

From this point on, Words, Inc., thought and worked in a different context. The company was able to introduce new changes throughout its business and industry.

And Words, Inc., is not alone. Companies like Microsoft and Honda are changing every day; however, the preponderance of companies continue to struggle with what and how to change.

Five Enduring Truths

This need for new thinking is not a rejection of what already is, nor is it a starting over. It is a *movement toward a much more powerful capability.* It's not another alternative program, an either-or approach, a derision of what has gone before, and it's not a "new and improved" business fad. Interestingly, the new thinking has some of its foundation in several of the natural, core truths that have emerged from the deluge of change efforts over the past decade.

We have learned a few things as we've traveled the road of change, embracing management theories as if they were road maps to the promised land. A glance in the rearview mirror reveals some lessons learned and a few enduring truths that we can adopt as working principles to be applied in the exploration of new thoughtware. We should take these core truths with us as we move forward, but not get stuck in all that surrounds them or worship the concepts as false idols. Rather, we need to glean the good and discard the chaff. New thoughtware embraces five enduring truths, as shown in Figure 3-1. Let's look at each of these principles of organization in detail.

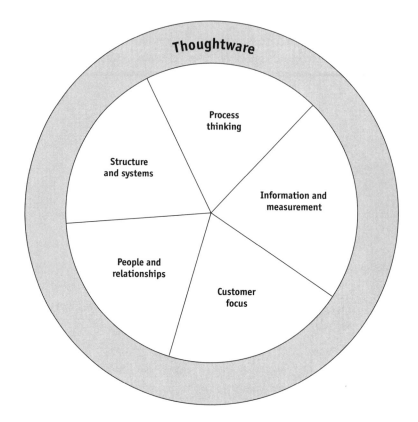

Figure 3-1. Five Core Truths

In Process Thinking Is Power

Process thinking is the embryo of process reengineering, the seed from which we set out to radically redesign our businesses. From this we discovered the primacy of *horizontalism* and the power of process over function. We now know the organization is a conglomerate of natural processes that reaches far beyond the borders of any department or the influence of any particular part. We now see the organization as a river, fluid and flowing, as opposed to a series of landlocked lakes. And, just as a river is tireless in its journey to the sea, so too the new organization must be tireless in the pursuit of its goal. It must never waiver from its mission, and it must continually change shape, size, and flow to facilitate every situation. Volume fluctuates. Boundaries move. Everything is flexible. Nothing is rigid, nothing is fixed. The core truth gleaned from reengineering is *the power of process and the irrefutable fact that process moves horizontally,* transcending boundaries, functions, and traditional structure. This universal thought is a keystone of new thoughtware.

Information and Measurement Are Life Sustaining

Under the rule of old thoughtware, information cripples us. Accounting departments give us scorecards, but what do they really tell us? MIS departments are burdened with old thoughtware and run by gatekeepers of information who oversee vast systems of data. *None* of this data means much when the information is born of old thoughtware. Most of our current measurement and reporting systems capture only 15 percent of the organization's cost drivers.[2] This is because old financial thinking and measuring techniques spew out bleached data that contains little or no performance measurement value. This data only monitors and reports (e.g., budgets, forecasts, cost centers, departmental comparisons) in an attempt to predict, control, and provide cause-and-effect ratios that have little to do with what is *really* happening in the organization. We have striven to analyze, analyze, analyze, digging for the cause of a problem when so many problems won't yield to more analysis.

Forget it. Take the information and look at it differently. Don't analyze it again, don't search for a cause, instead look for a different way to use the information.

Under the new thoughtware, total access to information is critical. Abundance, free flow, complexity, multiple interpretations: These are the watchwords of organizational information today. No longer should we try to inhibit or control information flow. We need to learn how to respond to it and create action around it.

New thoughtware looks for instability, conflict, ambiguity, and complexity and asks: Why is it so? What is the new information, the new context? How can we use this information to create new form, new substance? If knowledge is king, then information is the king's ransom—the source of growth and prosperity.

Getting valued information in the hands of the right people is imperative. Technology has made this easy, if we allow it to happen. We must see technology and computers for what they are—connectors that create unlimited access to data which can give us the power to change anything. Because of this, we need new thoughtware to reconfigure the context in which the information works and allow everyone to have panoramic access to information. Information is the raw material of knowledge and we can only access knowledge-processing with a measurement system that helps develop individual capability. We need to view the information in the entire system, not just a piece of it, so that everything is aligned with overall goals and everyone knows what to work on to achieve such alignment. This continually transforms information into value-added action. Give information to everyone. Give information every possibility, every interpretation, every viewpoint; in return, the organization will give back unlimited, unimagined solutions.

The Customer Is Central

It has been said that the moment of truth in any company is anytime or anywhere a customer is in contact with an employee. There are literally tens of thousands of such moments, and they define a company's customer focus more than anything else. It goes even further. It starts with thought-ware, because inherent in satisfying any customer is the thinking of every employee—imagining it, designing it, producing it, testing it, approving it, pricing it, delivering it, selling it, and servicing it. New thoughtware says, Everyone is available to the customer, anytime, anywhere.

> *Customer focus is a state of mind that has a direct bearing on every decision in the organization.*

Old thoughtware is based on the premise that we utilize our resources to satisfy the customer. It builds customer response systems around continuous, linear models that position the customer at the end of the supply chain, as the object to focus all efforts on (see Figure 3-2). But this alignment places too many people's thinking out of touch with the customer. And out of touch means out of focus.

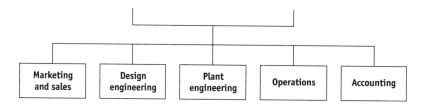

Figure 3-2. A Typical Departmental Structure

In contrast, new thoughtware sharpens the focus. More than that, it changes the focus and sees the customer at the center, not the end, of every process—at the core of all thoughts and activities. Instead of becoming a long, continuous line that reaches out to the customer, the organization configures into a discontinuous shape in which the customer is present everywhere, and touches everyone, all the time, as illustrated in Figure 3-3. Operating from this perspective, the organization can focus on the right customers and the right needs, and develop mutually successful partnering and working relationships. This intimate integration of the customer is fundamental in new thoughtware.

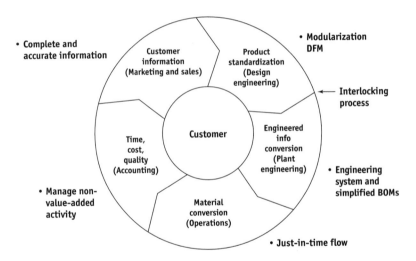

Figure 3-3. A Redesigned Customer-Centered Structure

People and Relationships Are Critical Assets

People, process, and participation create an intricate set of relationships that constitute the body and soul of the organization. And the quality of those relationships dictates the quality of the work life. We can no longer succeed just by managing the people, moving the parts, and controlling the processes. *We must manage the relationships,* and we must allow people to understand, design, and run the processes with unfettered and uncontrolled participation. We must allow people to reach their own entitlement in pursuit of the organization's entitlement (entitlement is that point of achievement that people can reach through maximum use of their current potential and optimum use of the organization's available resources).

> *You can't legislate participation. It makes no more sense than trying to automate rework.*

For years senior management tried to empower employees, as if a few edicts and the right techniques would empower the people and all would be changed. Then they realized that empowerment, dictated from on high, didn't take at the grass roots. Empowerment is old thoughtware. It implies that someone can bestow power upon someone else. This might be so in the old organizational structures where power is jealously controlled at the top, but in an information-free, knowledge-hungry environment (the new context), new structures form around access to information and those who have access have power, granted or not. In the past rush to empowerment we came up short because we failed to integrate other crucial areas that go hand in hand with empowerment: skills, authority, accountability, and measurement. What we have done is tinker with some, but not all, of these ingredients; thus creating nothing more than a dangerous, self-destructing program within a never-changing organizational context. Empowerment is ill-defined and has been created out of context.

New thoughtware focuses on *allowment,* not as a change in semantics, but as a contextual change. It's about understanding the reallocation of power, breaking down old controls, and designing organizations around relationships that create new autonomies, provide open access, and *allow* for growth in capability and accountability. It's about employees as capital assets. It's thinking of people as assets on the balance sheet, not as an expense, providing them with whatever it takes (information, skills, and authority) to manage the organization's capacity, and then *allowing* them to do so.

> *Power in organizations is the capacity*
> *generated by relationships.*
> —M. WHEATLEY

Structure and Systems Reflect Purpose

If processes are fluid, relationships are everything, and information is everywhere, then where are our organizational structures and systems? Nowhere—or somewhere in the past. Most of them are stuck in old thoughtware, still encumbered by hierarchies, controls, and rigid systems. It's a type of rigor mortis. In truth, most of our traditional structures have been dead for years.

Future-thinking organizations cannot be defined easily or structured easily. Nor should they be. They, and the forces that define them, are in a constant state of flux—moving, shifting, shaping, and facilitating processes and relationships. Obstinately, traditional organizations (built on old thoughtware) are forever trying to improve on the existing structure. They want to change it, fix it, tune it, tweak it because they believe *what is* is not *what should be.* Wrong thought! *What is* is okay. The current structure *is* working, based on the current relationships, processes, and systems. Leave it. Don't try to change it. Don't sweat the structure. Look at what creates it and change that.

> *Organizational structure is always*
> *the result of relationships,*
> *not the cause of them.*

New thoughtware views structure not as a cause, but as a result. It leaves the structure where it is and moves on. New thoughtware deals with *what is to be,* and moves to *where you want to be,* knowing the structure will follow. Organizational structure is seen as a provider, not a dictator. Its purpose is to form itself to the new systems, new relationships, and new processes.

> *Our current measurement systems tell us exacting*
> *information that is largely irrelevant to managing the*
> *organization, is seldom linked to strategic direction,*
> *and impedes rather than facilitates.*

The future does not call for the annihilation of current structures. The concern is for the inherent systems that create the structure. These systems, which are based on the need to provide organization, information, order, skills, and authority, must change, and this is where we must apply new thoughtware. Change financial systems to count what really counts, measurement systems to measure what really matters, information systems to give everybody all the information, learning systems to be broad enough and deep enough to sustain the organization far into the future, compensation systems to pay people for doing what needs to be done instead of just for doing their jobs. As Elliott Jaques maintains in *Human Capability,* we must have an employee system and an accountability hierarchy that allows everyone to find and pursue their maximum capability. There must be structure, but it must reflect and match the natural hierarachy inherent in employees' current and potential capability.[3] In turn, the need is to provide support systems that can deliver the information, order (not control), skills, authority, and hierarchy where they're needed and when they're needed in order to generate real value. To deliver *whatever is necessary* to engage the future competently, every day, structures must serve this higher purpose.

New thoughtware creates new action. It *precedes* the structure. By acting, you create new form—form that supports and assists, structures that facilitate, not impede. Only new thoughtware can generate such structure.

Historical Thoughts

In addition to these five enduring truths there are several other essential carry-forwards in the development of new thoughtware, some of which go back to the thinking of Aristotle. Aristotle's work put forward a set of requirements (called context) to allow for the proper, scientific demonstration of all natural processes (in our words: *the context in which things are developed is critical to the outcome*). Ever since, this principle has been accepted as an instrument of thought, a means of reasoning. It was known collectively as *Organumi,* or *Thoughtware.*

Centuries later, in 1620, Sir Francis Bacon created the treatise *Novum Organum* (New Thoughtware) to provide formal context to the intangible instrument known as scientific method. Descartes then argued in *Discourse on Method* that you must have rational assumptions *in context* to understand the principles of natural science (in our words: *if you don't consider the context in which you try to change things, the applied content will change very little*). Descartes further proffered that all phenomena must be studied "without a dogmatic adherence to the past."[4] So what we're trying to get at is not new, and yet it is still widely ignored.

In addition to context, another historical fact that is ignored is the thinking on which organizations are designed. In *Future Perfect,* Stanley Davis argues that there is a logical progression from scientific discovery to the creation of our 20th century organizations.[5] We transform scientific understanding into new technologies. Then we use the technologies to create business products and services, and then we design organizations to produce the products and services. Creating the organization is the *last* step in the process. Davis points out that the lag time is extremely long between the scientific understanding and the development of the new technologies, products, and services and the formation of the organization. Organizational thinking in the 1990s is still rooted in the scientific laws of the 17th, 18th, 19th, and early 20th centuries.

We have built today's organizations by combining the scientific thinking of Sir Isaac Newton (the working of the parts provides an understanding of the whole), the economic thinking of Adam Smith (*Wealth of Nations* and economies of scale), the manufacturing thinking of Frederick Taylor (optimized time-in-motion, unit costs, and assembly line efficiency), and the modern management thinking of Alfred Sloan (decentralizing operations while centralizing policies, finance, etc.). All of this thinking has provided the foundation for unparalleled industrial development. It has been the primary means of organizing businesses through the first 75 years of this century, but now, rampant new technology has changed everything—violently and forever. Our organizations are being propelled into a whole new context for which they were not designed and with which they cannot cope.

Notes

[1] Paul Zane Pilzer, *Unlimited Wealth* (New York: Crown Publishers, 1990), p. 6.

[2] H. Thomas Johnson and Robert S. Kaplan, *Relevance Lost* (Boston: Harvard Business School Press, 1991).

[3] Elliott Jaques and Kathryn Cason, *Human Capability* (Falls Church, VA: Cason Hall and Company, 1994).

[4] René Descartes, *Discourse on Method* (London: Dent, 1957).

[5] Stanley Davis, *Future Perfect* (Reading, MA: Addison-Wesley, 1987).

The Drivers of New Context | 4

The universe begins to look more like
a great thought than a great machine.

—ASTRONOMER JAMES JEAN, 1930

Does history repeat itself? You bet it does, over and over again. Good news, bad news, no news, new news; regardless, time moves on, change happens, and history repeats. It's not a question of whether history is good or bad; it's a question of whether we get better or worse because of it. Of course, we like to think that we get better, and there's plenty of evidence that we do learn from history. Yet there's plenty of evidence to the contrary, as well. And nowhere is the contrary more obvious than in our business organizations, those venerable institutions we spend such an inordinate amount of time, money, and effort working to change for the better.

Much has been written about scientific discovery, economic models, management theory, and organizational design, but little of it has been tied together in the examination of organizational behavior, structure, and performance. In recent years considerable new thinking has been expressed in works by such thinkers as Stanley Davis (*Future Perfect*); Margaret Wheatley (*Leadership and the New Science*); Edward de Bono (*Serious Creativity* and *Teach Yourself to Think*); Peter Senge (*The Fifth Discipline*); Gary Hamel and C.K. Prahalad (*Competing for the Future*); Kevin Kelly (*Out of Control*); Nuala Beck (*Shifting Gears* and *Excelerate*); Paul Zane Pilzer (*Unlimited Wealth*); Richard T. Pascale (*Managing on the Edge*); Peter Drucker (*Managing in a Time of Great Change*); and Henry Mintzberg (*The Rise and Fall of Strategic Planning*) among others. In addition, the far-reaching work of Elliott Jaques (*Requisite Organization, Human Capability, Executive Leadership, The Form of Time, A General Theory of Bureaucracy*) has provided unparalleled insight and scientific findings over five decades. But even with all of this provocative thinking, we can't seem to get very far. In fact, we're still tied, by some invisible line, to centuries of old thinking.

As we said at the end of the previous chapter, the seed of today's organizational thinking stretches back over three centuries of study, and although much has changed in the field of science since Newton, little of substance has changed in the field of organizational thinking. Beyond the handful of thinkers mentioned above, and perhaps a few more, we are awash in a tsunami of specious techniques and technocrats spewing forth concepts, tools, and bafflegab in the subjective (too often avaricious) pursuit of solutions. We *must* explore beyond the obvious, the latest, and the convenient, to find the cornerstones and genesis of change.

The Genesis of New Context

The development of our future organizations must be in concert with, and learn from, the scientific and *new* socio-economic thinking that is postulated by the minds of Elliott Jaques and Margaret Wheatley. This is critical to understanding the new context in which we must operate. In her book *Leadership and the New Science,* Wheatley looks at the interconnectedness of systems, relationships, and information, and opens the windows of our mind to the similarities between the natural sciences and organizational structure and function. And nowhere is profound, scientifically-based thinking more evident than in the findings of Jaques, who has pursued the application of the natural sciences in exploding age-old assumptions and in challenging every management-change concept.

What Jaques has developed is a body of work, spread over 50 years, that is solidly based on scientific study and empirical findings, and provides undisputed theory on which to look at the organization of work and people. This kind of thinking allows us to look far more objectively at the driving forces forming organizations, as well as the new context in which they must survive. It allows us to see, perhaps for the first time, how limiting old thoughtware really is.

The Drivers of New Context

As the ever-changing, external context continues to buffet and batter our organizations, it has exposed four fundamental drivers and creators of new context. Shown in Figure 4-1 as the forces that will take us from old thoughtware to new, they are relationships; information; speed, flexibility, and focus; and accountability. These are the dominant characteristics, the principles that form the new context in which organizations must live and operate.

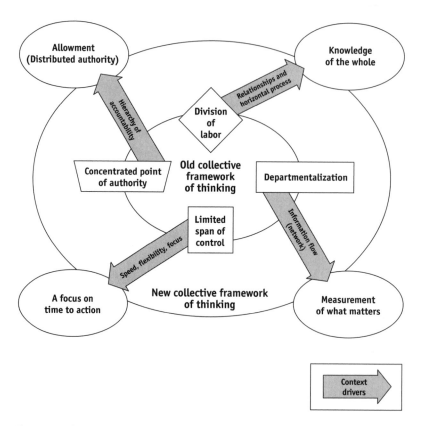

Figure 4-1. The Drivers of New Context

Relationships

There is no shortage of books and advice on relationships. Relationship marketing, relationship selling, relationship management, relationship banking—it's a whole school of thought unto itself. And with organizations, it's also a major relearning for managers. For decades we trained to be managers of departments and functions, but few of us have trained to manage relationships—those intangible, undefined spaces between functions and departments, employee and employee, employee and customer, employee and supplier. Relationships are the "white spaces" between the boxes on organization charts. The problem is no one manages the white spaces. Whether they are team relationships, where everyone reports to each other, or manager–subordinate relationships, *relationships are everything.* Relationships are the connections, the interactions, the reactions, the actions, the energy, the impetus, the processes, and the cause and the effect. Relationships can also be the limitations on all of these.

For centuries we have focused on the parts (the functions), assuming that if we know everything there is to know about every part (the type of specialization that leads to division of labor), then we will understand and be able to manage the whole. So we dissect, analyze, and build our organizations according to the parts. We produce by having one part impact on another part and another part, and so on. This is old, Newtonian thought.

But when we look at more advanced science, we find that quantum theory advocates do not focus on the parts (particles), but rather on the relationships *among* the particles. A premise of quantum theory is that it cannot predict the behavior of any individual particle. Instead, it deals in terms of the relative probability of the future position (and velocity) of a particle. This is the kind of thinking we must apply in our organizations, where even the probability isn't very probable. We must build the relationships that allow the organization to be extremely flexible and adaptable. We must understand and describe the organization by its relationships, not by objectives, functions, and departments. The assumptions that people in the organization hold about themselves, and how they work together, must focus on how to orchestrate the flow of their relationships rather than the walls that separate them.

One way of looking at relationships in an organization is to build a relationship map such as the one shown in Figure 4-2. Taking the place of a traditional organizational chart (which tells us nothing), a relationship map is built by the process of dialogue among the different functions in the organization. It sets out how "we really operate." It tells us how product flows, who the customer is, where the customer is, and where the non-value-added activity is. It exposes the lack of full knowledge of the whole process. It allows people to start thinking about the organization as a series of relationships, not a series of reporting lines. It's important to note that old thoughtware considers "mapping" as a product, an output, while new thoughtware sees that the process, not the end product, is what is most important.

Relationships must become the overriding principle of organizational thinking. We must think about people's relationships with each other, the organization, the customers, the suppliers, and the surrounding environment. With a focus on the aggregate of the relationships and on the organization's core competencies, we can begin to mold things in concert with the ever-moving, ever-changing system we call an organization. So, stop managing the parts and start managing the relationships. Stop damming-up the parts and managing the lakes; instead, open the dams and manage the whole river.

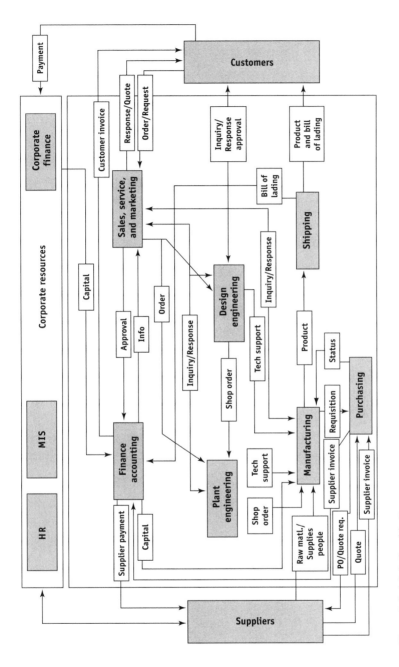

Figure 4-2. A Relationship Map

Information Flow

Information is the basis of the universe.
—JOHN WHEELER, PHYSICIST

Information becomes knowledge, and as Alvin Toffler suggests in his book *Powershift,* knowledge is critical in the struggle for power in the new world and the key to moving into the new context. Technology has changed the rules of the game. Now we must handle both the abundance of information and the speed at which information is available in order to manage in the new context. The old thoughtware calls this "information overload." The new thoughtware considers it "access to unlimited opportunity."

The information supply available to us doubles every five years.
—RICHARD SAUL WURMAN

Information is a potentially powerful force. If we are to face the future with any chance of success, then there must be total access to information, a wide-open Information Highway that connects and reaches into every corner of the organization. Because information represents potential power, one of the most highly developed skills—and consequently one of the most constraining habits within an organization—is the tendency to harbor and limit access to information. This is a huge handicap. Information must be shared openly and used by everyone, at every point in the organization, so that quick response can be made to every valid demand.

Remove the barriers created by delay, misinformation, or no information. Become fast, not by running faster but by moving information faster and farther than ever before. Remove the hurdles that retard the movement and sharing of information. In a world where we can move money from Singapore to Amsterdam to Moscow to New York to Chicago in seconds, it's rather obvious that information and the speed with which it is transferred are driving imperatives of the new context.

Speed, Flexibility, and Focus

The organization in the new context must be fast, flexible, and focused. These are not the only attributes needed to move an organization beyond the horizon and allow it to stake a claim in the future, but without them the horizon will be a fast-fading mirage.

Speed

Speed does not mean setting the world record in the 100-meter dash of business every time out of the blocks. It does mean being able to respond faster than the competition. Speed is a point of differentiation, just as quality, value, and profitability—now givens—once were. Without speed, the race is lost. But it is a subjective measure; it only counts when the customer *considers* you speedy. It means responding when, where, and how the customer wants. It means removing every possible impediment in an attempt to eliminate the choking burden of non-value activity and win the race for customer satisfaction. Understand, speed is about availability, *not* utilization. It's not simply cycle time reduction, it's flexibility. For example, not everyone wants or will pay for "one-hour photos," but it *is* available if wanted!

As an example of the impact of speed, consider that in the traditional timeline of new product development, companies make scores of changes, all of which take time and cause a slower (and perhaps less than perfect) product launch (see Figure 4-3). The only way to lead the competition is to eliminate the non-value-adding steps in the process, compress the time frame, and get it right before launch.

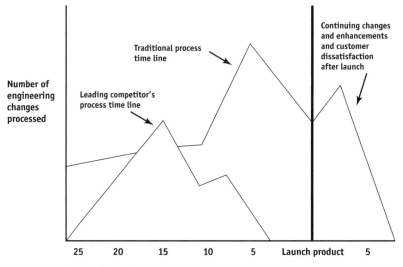

Data source: American Supplier Institute

Figure 4-3. How Does Our Time Compare to the Competitor's?

In some industries fast has already become a given. Courier services, news networks, fast food, and photo development are players who must continually maintain speed while finding other points of differentiation. However, in the great majority of businesses, being fast is still a wishful thought. There are just too many steps (hurdles and non-value-added time) involved in getting the product or service to the customer. Consider the ratio of value-added time to actual activity (steps) in the industries shown in Figure 4-4.

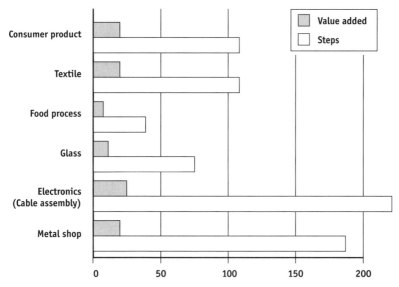

Data source: *Cycle Time Management* by P. Northey and N. Southway

Figure 4-4. Cycle Time Activity Analysis

Flexibility

The future is unforgiving. If you cannot meet it on *its* terms, you won't be there. Time-to-market, response time, and solve-it time are shrinking at an incredible rate. Be fast or be last. But being fast requires flexibility. Responsiveness is an opportunity that can only be achieved if the organization as a whole is flexible, with the capability to change on the run, in flight, in motion, immediately. Opportunities, problems, conflicts, issues, and decisions can only be handled quickly if the organization is incredibly flexible. In a world where change takes place at such high velocity, mere survival depends on adaptability and systems that can deal with constant change.

In business, systems have been the backbone of organization, essential to our growth. But systems have become a double-edged sword in that they cause conformity and rigidity.

As we search for new ways to respond to the speed of change, our systems must become much more flexible. The old systems were designed to link and manage the parts, much like a system of lakes with many islands (islands of departmental knowledge or specialized technology) and connecting control dams (finance departments, MIS). The new systems, however, must serve the whole, like a constantly moving river with no dam controls. And new systems do not control the river; rather, they form with it as it moves ahead with no barriers (divisions or islands of information). Studies of natural systems in the universe show that they are amorphous, fluid entities that are highly capable of adapting and shaping themselves to the environmental circumstances (demands) around them. This natural capability to adjust, flow, and respond is precisely what is required in our new organizations.

> • By Land, by Sea, by Air, by Bicycle—Your Choice! •
> It used to be that when you needed a package delivered, you took it to the Post Office and chose between first class, second class, or bulk rate. In return, the Post Office gave you this guarantee: the package will get through. The only question was when? Tomorrow? Next week? Next month? But now courier services have leapt into global prominence with flexibility and speed as their points of differentiation. The courier will come to your office and collect the package from you. They will also give you a dozen or so options for sending your package anywhere you want—and nearly anytime you want. "Same day" service can mean immediate, rush, A.M./P.M., or regular. "Tomorrow" can mean delivery by 8 A.M., 10 A.M., or 3 P.M. Or you can choose to have your package delivered in two or three days. It's all your choice, not the deliverer's. *That's* flexibility.

Competitive advantage occurs once your value-delivery system is two to three times more flexible and faster than your competitor's.

Flexibility means temporary. Teams, projects, and structures must be capable of fast formation and sudden disbandment. Flexibility also means now. It means what is today is not tomorrow, and it knows that yesterday was years ago. Today in some organizations we are beginning to see what flexibility really means. Files on wheels, files on an intranet, outsourcing, networking, partnering, collaborating, connecting, disconnecting, and being there—wherever *there* is.

Focus

It's been said many times, but done so seldom: "Focus on core competencies and do not try to be all things to all people." This is not a new concept, but knowing it, and doing it, are usually mind-years apart. Focusing on core competencies and what they mean to an organization must become a common way of thinking, one that builds around a growth strategy and is adopted by everyone in the organization—with the right thoughtware. Focus impacts everything, from a focus on customers and the allocation of resources to meet their needs, to a focus by employees on doing the tasks that only add value to the value-delivery system. We must refocus on these two major assets: customers and employees.

By looking through a more focused lens we can often see a different picture. When the picture looks different we may decide to do exactly the opposite of what we might normally do. For example, instead of downsizing employees, we might downsize customers. Why? Because focus dictates that we

Ask yourself the question, "If my customer knew I was doing this, would they pay for it?"

don't try to be all things to all people (many companies have grown by getting rid of customers), and downsizing employees throws out one of the very ingredients of our core competencies. New thoughtware is critical to new focus, and it can help prevent us from drastically undermining the all-important corporate annuity for growth—loyal customers, loyal employees, and continually improving core competencies.

• SORRY, WE HAVE NO BANANAS OR HOT DOGS •

Hamburgers, hotdogs, french fries, soft drinks, ice cream cones, banana splits, chicken, pizza—all part of the world's fast-food smorgasbord, but some of them you *won't* find at McDonald's, the undisputed billionaire king of fast food. McDonald's say, "Yes, we have no bananas and no hot dogs." Why? Because of focus. The thinking behind the fast-food giant's focus is not as obvious, but you can rest assured there is some solid thinking. McDonald's knows its core competencies, trains its people accordingly, and stays focused and fast.

The company even forgoes some flexibility to ensure speed. That's focus. (McDonald's didn't get into the pizza business until they knew they were fully entitled to do so).

Another example of changing focus from a functional, departmentalized system to a customer-focused, cross-functional system can be seen in the rethinking and subsequent reorganization of a public utility. Old thinking meant installation orders bounced around in separate departments, in different locations, and on different floors in the same building (see Figure 4-5). The order followed linear, function-by-function steps to and through the various departments-of-knowledge (generation, transmission, research and development, marketing, and customer service) until the order was fulfilled. Normally, it took about 130 days to install a new industrial customer.

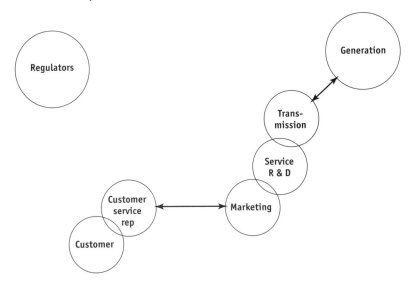

Figure 4-5. A Functionally Focused Power Utility Company

When the utility company installed new thoughtware, however, it created a lot of change and a lot of customer satisfaction (along with a lot of upheaval). Figure 4-6 visually represents the reorganization in one particular district. Each district was set up in one location, on one floor, with all the relevant, cross-functional people focused on the customer. The previously long, arduous, pass-along-and-wait process was radically compressed, communications were greatly improved, and new customers were installed in about 25 days.

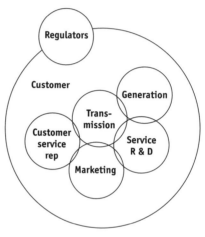

Figure 4-6. A Customer-Focused Power Utility Company

Hierarchy of Accountability

Elliott Jaques defines what he calls *accountability hierarchy* and unequivocally states that there can be *no* organizational order or consistent performance without it. Jaques also shatters the myth that being accountable in some way implies being autocratic. It does not. Accountability is fundamental to leadership at any level and has nothing to do with being autocratic; however, our fear of being overly autocratic too often translates into a fear of being accountable. So, individual accountability, and the requisite hierarchy between people that goes hand-in-hand with it, gets lost in the misconception that hierarchy is bureaucracy. It is not. Jaques explains that the hierarchy of accountability must form around a clear manager–subordinate relationship, and be based on the degree of task complexity in the work to be done and on the individual's capability to process such complexity.[1] Without this there is pervasive dysfunction.

Accountability requires measurement. As illustrated in Figure 4-7, a complete measurement hierarchy begins at the top with the determination of the core values that require measurement. In this case, the core values are performance, people, customers, innovation, and technology. The core values are then further broken down into attributes that must be measured in order to transform the intangibility of the values. In this case, for instance, the core value, *customers,* can be broken into the

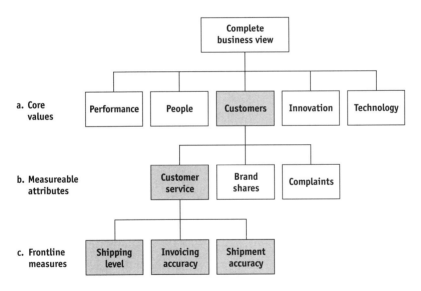

Figure 4-7. The Measurement Hierarchy

attribute, *customer service.* Finally, the measurement hierarchy flows down to the front lines of the organization in order to connect real-time performance to the overarching values and goals of the organization. In this example, customer service (an attribute of the core value customers) can be tangibly measured in such tasks as shipping level, invoicing accuracy, and shipment accuracy.

Accountability has four, easy-to-recognize dimensions: output, measurement, authority, and skills. The dimension *output* is the opposite of input, or activities. Take a moment from reading this book and try an exercise. Describe, in one minute, your job. What do you do? Perhaps you manage people, write letters, sign contracts, ship products, or administer policies. Now take another minute and describe your job again, but this time do not use a verb. People, letters, contracts, shipments, and policies are output, the products of your job. This is what you're accountable for.

The second dimension is *measurement,* the means to let you know how well you are doing. To understand this concept, imagine you are working in isolation for a year, talking with no one. If, when the year is up, someone asked you to describe how you could tell if you had done well and been effective, what would be your answer? That is what should be measured.

The third breakpoint in accountability is what we call *point of authority.* When authority is not where the accountability is, it doesn't work. Authority can range from making recommendations (for which there must be the right response structure) to just doing it; either way, the point of authority and accountability must be in the same place.

The last, but not the least, dimension is *skills.* Accountability without proper skills is certain failure. It's obvious that no one can be held accountable if they do not have the skills to handle the task.

Hierarchy without the right structure of accountability is like a body without a skeleton. We must rethink, rework, and redesign our organizations with a much different view of accountability and the need for the right hierarchy.

Shifts in these four drivers of context—relationships, information, speed, and accountability—are altering the landscape, obliterating the rules, and tilting the playing field of business. It's up to every organization that wants to compete to fully understand the new context. It's about knowing, measuring, responding, and allowing the organization to *think differently.* Only then can it move to, and deal with, new context.

Note

[1] Elliott Jacques and Kathryn Cason, *Human Capability* (Falls Church, VA: Cason Hall and Company, 1994).

new
thoughtware

Paradigm-Breaking Thoughts | 5

If a cat spoke, it would say things like,
"Hey, I don't see the problem here."

—Roy Blount, Jr.

Not seeing the problem is the problem. We have developed an overly myopic view that thinks it sees the problem, but totally misses the context in which the problem exists. Seeing the *context,* on the other hand, puts the real problem in perspective and often allows one to move beyond tactical problem solving to a totally new direction. It needs thinking that notices what is not being noticed and illuminates context. To break through into new context we need drastic changes in the fundamental way we think about our organizations.

• I Thought... Why? •

"Good-bye." "Good-bye." "Thank you." "Good-bye." "Thank you." "Good-bye."

This is *not* good-bye, I thought as I left the airplane to the metronome-like good-byes of the flight attendants. And I shouldn't really say thank you until I'm sure this has been a good trip. I'm only leaving the airplane, not the airline. I'm still with Old Context Airlines right through the airport, customs, baggage claim, and out the turnstile. So why are they telling me good-bye? I guess *they* think it's good-bye. But why? Maybe because they're thinking about their job and not about what's next for the customer. They're not noticing what's not being noticed.

I pick up my rental car. "Thank you, sir. Here are your keys. The license number of your car is 236 KMV. Our driver will take you right to your car."

"Where's your express drop off? I have a 1:50 flight tomorrow and I'll be running tight."

"You'll see the large, green Rental Car Return signs as you enter the airport, sir. Just follow them and our attendants will meet you, take the keys, run your account through the computer, and have you on your way in less than a minute."

"Great! Do I get charged an extra half day for returning a couple of hours over 24 hours?"

"We charge you for the exact hours used, sir. Nothing more."

"Thank you." Walking out of the airport I thought about how easy it was to have a rental car available any time night or day and I could check in or out 24 hours a day. That availability is important to me.

As I pulled up in front of my hotel the hotel courtesy van was just pulling away. But as I stopped, so did the van. The driver hopped out and came to greet me.

"Good morning, sir. Let me give you a hand with your bag."

"Thank you." As we entered the lobby, I noticed the doorman busily tagging about a dozen bags that must have belonged to a group checking in. Over at the reception counter one couple was checking in and another man was checking out. Both front-desk personnel were busy with these people. As I settled in behind the young couple, the van driver set my bag down and stepped behind the counter.

"Let me check you in, sir." I looked around slightly surprised. He is talking to me ... but he's the *van driver*. Perplexed but pleased, I stepped up to the counter.

He punched up the computer, confirmed my reservation, took an imprint of my credit card, got my signature, and welcomed me by name. "You'll be in room 1517 and I'll bring your bags up, sir." He was out from behind the counter in a flash, leading me to the elevators. As we passed the doorman, they spoke.

"Al, I'm finished tagging these bags so I'll run over to the airport for the next pickup."

My van driver-front desk clerk-become bellhop replied. "Good, I'll get those bags loaded and cover the front. See you in 20 minutes." He turned to me. "Sir, I'll park your car and leave the keys at the front desk for you."

I was checked in and up to my room in less than three minutes. And surprise, surprise, the room was made up and ready even though it was only 10:00 A.M. I thought, now that's customer-first service with a real difference. Why?

I plugged in my laptop and made a few calls. After talking with my office I decided to change my scheduled flight home from tomorrow afternoon to tomorrow evening. Before booking the flight I thought I'd better inquire about checkout time. I could always leave at checkout time and work in the airport lounge after my meeting. I called the front desk. "Hello, can you tell me when checkout time is?"

"There is no checkout time, sir. It's whenever you leave."

"But it'll cost me an extra day if I stay until five or six, won't it?"

"No sir. You'll just be charged for the hours you stay with us, based on your room rate. And you need not notify us, just check out whenever you want."

"Thank you *very* much." As I hung up the phone I thought, "Wow! Why can't every hotel be like that?"

The stark contrasts of these everyday events intrigued me. Some were subtle, some significant. As I dined that evening at a highly recommended restaurant—with prices to match—I began to observe the organization around me. Why did the maitre d' seat me, then never appear again? Why did the waiter take my food order, but the wine steward my wine order? And then the waiter cleared my place, but didn't refill my wine glass. The wine steward refilled my wine glass, but not my water glass—I had to wait for the waiter for the water (I thought the waiter was supposed to do the waiting, not me). Well, it *is* highly recommended, highly priced, highly organized, and highly efficient—but from their perspective, not the customers'. What could they be thinking? Whatever it is, some of them are thinking very *differently* than others.

Paradigm Busting

Old habits die hard and old thinking is like an addiction. The task before us is to exorcise deeply imbedded operating principles and replace them with new principles—founded on new thoughtware.

> *Each and every bad habit must be*
> *replaced by a good habit.*
> —OG MANDINO

Old thoughtware is everywhere. It's pervasive, normal, everyday, accepted thinking. It masquerades as efficiency and necessity: we-need-that-report, we've-always-done-it-that-way, the-boss-said-so, the-customer-asked-for-it, and just-because. The principles of old thoughtware—division of labor, departmentalization, limited span of control, and concentrated point of authority—must go! They are no longer relevant in the new context, and the drivers of the new context require quite different thoughtware. *Knowledge, measurement, time to action,* and *allowment* must replace them (see Figure 5-1). Understanding each major component of the new thoughtware is the starting gate for major change. As we introduce each component, notice how it replaces its old thoughtware counterparts. Also notice the corresponding context drivers for each new component. We'll discuss each component in detail in the coming chapters.

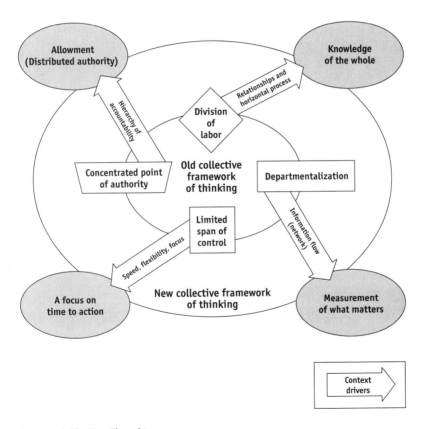

Figure 5-1. The New Thoughtware

Knowledge of the Whole (Renders Division of Labor Obsolete)

Division of labor is based on the outdated need to achieve economic advantage by organizing around specialization. But yesterday's economic advantage is giving way to today's relentless demand to respond faster and faster. Today, with relationships as the driver, we have the potential to develop knowledge anywhere, to cross-train, cross-functionalize, and cross over any borders, boundaries, or functional boxes. Until we replace departmentalization with knowledge of the whole, the information and expertise we need to develop new knowledge remains locked up in isolated functions, specialties, and heads.

New thoughtware destroys old barriers and leaps old hurdles. It dismisses old thinking and lets us have knowledge of the whole, as well as our own specialization, and allows us to think across all boundaries. It's disruptive and creative at the same time. It creates a new context in which we thrive on information, thirst for knowledge, and see new, previously unconsidered possibilities. The convergence and divergence of information can create unprecedented new knowledge, and with knowledge we transcend old boundaries. Technology slams the point of information convergence deep into every organization and makes the division of labor obsolete. Everyone now has the potential to understand and contribute to a far greater portion of the whole than ever before.

• LIGHTS, ACTION ... OOPS,
ENGINEERING CHANGED THE LIGHTS — AGAIN •

General Motors' development of the Chevy Lumina is an illuminating story. The Lumina was designed in the mid-1980s to compete with Japanese imports (a novel, but late-blooming idea) and was finally ready for the market in 1991. Even though the competition managed to go through four redesigns in the same period and Mazda's Miata was successfully brought out in just 18 months, General Motors was still operating under the old thoughtware, working through a labyrinth of departments, functions, and sequential processes. Design engineering worked separately from production engineering and in isolation from manufacturing. Design engineering constantly focused on optimizing the engineering and specifying the design to death. Theirs was the traditional silo mindset based on specialization and division of labor.

In addition to the obvious cost inefficiencies, this myopic thinking also created higher direct costs. At the time, GM was getting offshore quotations for parts. One very competitive quote for the Lumina's radio came from a Japanese supplier. The quote was never accepted because it never crossed over the silo walls. Purchasing knew there was an addendum to the quote offering a 20 percent reduction in the cost if one of design engineering's particular specifications was removed. But to the rigid thinking in purchasing this was unacceptable—after all, specs are specs. As such, no one from purchasing ever bothered to confer with anyone from design engineering to see if the spec in question—*that the radio could operate under water*—could be removed. So the better quote was rejected and the Lumina cost more. All because no one had the right knowledge in the right place to make the right decision.

Not until GM started to change its thinking did it change its ways. GM is where it is today (and that's still a long way from where it should be) because it has not dissolved decades of old thoughtware on specialization and division of labor. And progress is slow. Just ask Roger Smith, if you can find him.[1]

Knowledge will prevail. Divisions may continue to win some skirmishes and a few battles, but knowledge will win the war. And the greatest weapon available to build knowledge is new thoughtware. It can change the landscape forever.

> *Knowledge is becoming our most important product.*
> *This calls for different organizations, as well as*
> *different kinds of workers.*
> —PETER F. DRUCKER

Measurement of What Matters (Disintegrates Departmentalization)

The power of departmentalization has atrophied the overall organization by putting the goals of the department above those of the corporation. Silos, walls, barriers, and responsibilities have all grown from departmental functions that no longer meet the needs of the customer or the organization. Many senior executives still stand firm on this rickety platform. They still protect their departmental power base by limiting the involvement of their best people on cross-functional teams or by failing to resolve conflicts between departmental objectives and broader organizational goals. Many executives believe teams and cross-functionality are something that happens down the line, below them. So what we get is a strong identification with the culture of departmentalization and departmentalized motivation and measurement. Even process-complete departments, which numerous organizations have instituted, don't work if the measurements being used are not born of new thoughtware.

Many measurement systems are based on an old economy, an old organization, and old thoughtware. Such systems evaluate, but they don't help navigate. A new measurement hierarchy (with accountability and relevant motivational measures) must replace departmental hierarchy and provide a true navigational capability for the entire organization. Navigation means having the measurements that can tell you *where the organization is, where it's going, what it must do to get there, and how far on or off course it is.*

New thoughtware gets at *real* measurement, which is directly linked to the key factors that drive motivation, and tie it to meaningful organizational purpose, relevant objectives, and a common approach. It recognizes that the strongest motivator is a clear objective, easily measured and effectively tied to accountability and reward. For years though, we've measured what's easy, controllable, and "dollarizable"—labor efficiencies, utilization of machinery, and financial things that conform to the accounting architecture (e.g., ROI, RONA). But more than 50 percent of all measurement objectives are in conflict with each other, and most measurements capture only 15 percent of the real cost drivers.[2] Consequently, we have not found a very effective or meaningful way of measuring things that really matter, like flexibility, customer satisfaction, waste, and responsiveness. These things are not easily dollarized or measured, but they are directly related to the customer and the employees—*the* core assets. The only way to provide the opportunity for superb performance and significant contribution is to have the right measurements, link them to the company's objectives, and make them meaningful to the people doing the work.

> *If you're not measuring the right things, you're just practicing. You're not in the game yet.*

Speed, complexity, costs, competition, and demand have all changed the game. It's a game that old departments can no longer compete in and traditional measurement systems cannot support. Many unmeasured things now need measures. This requires new thoughtware, with information flow as its driver, to change the fixated, departmentalized mindset.

• WHO BLEW UP THE R&D DEPARTMENT? •

A major adhesives manufacturer in the Northeast U.S. (we'll call them Stick & Stay, Inc.) was facing declining market share and eroding margins. Stick & Stay, Inc., had to be more innovative—no, actually it was innovative, just not very fast. Its products were excellent and its customers included several Fortune 500 companies. But, as its customers intensified the fight for competitive advantage, they demanded more products with more and more innovation, faster and faster. The proliferation of products in the market meant that Stick & Stay, Inc., had to find a way to deliver "mass customization."

Traditionally, Stick & Stay could bring new products to market in 6 to 24 months (6 months for enhancements, 24 months for new product designs). That timeline was no longer good enough, but the R&D department was swamped and there seemed to be no reasonable solution. Then, in search of new ideas, the company formed a cross-functional team, which reported to an executive vice-president or approval body (no departmental blockage), to look at the problem. Soon, the team had gone beyond just generating ideas and moved into a whole new way of thinking. Knowing the company didn't have the capacity (in R&D) to handle the demand in anywhere near the time it had to, and because they had all the right people on the team with authority and resources to do whatever was necessary then, the team began to act on its thinking.

It was simultaneous because it had to be. The cross-functionality of the team allowed the members to place priorities on every R&D request *and* reallocate resources accordingly. The team began to filter the swamp of requests through the prioritization process, and as it prioritized, it also acted. The departmental pass-offs between marketing and R&D disappeared. Engineering, manufacturing, purchasing, and finance were involved at the very beginning of the process so knowledge and ideas traded hands in real time. Soon, the turnaround time spiraled downward. The company never resurrected the old R&D department. It wasn't necessary. The new process was called "Introtech," and in less than a year Stick & Stay, Inc., was introducing new products in 9 months and product enhancements in 1 month.

Bring down the barriers. Break out of the silos. Banish the departments. Focus on process, install cross-functionality at *every* level, and create a relevant context in which you can correctly measure what matters, what really drives the process.

A Focus on Time to Action (Makes Span of Control Redundant)

Time is an asset, not an enemy. If we see time in the right context we can see why our perceived need for bureaucratic control is not only unnecessary, but severely damaging. With time as the crucible in which we think and operate, old thoughtware can be seen for what it is: a relic of the past. Time is a driving force. Decision making and action are imperative. And they cannot be managed properly in the inhibiting hierarchy of span of control.

A flat organization doesn't mean one layer, just as hierarchy doesn't mean a dozen layers. What hierarchy does mean is accountability that *allows*. What works best *is* best. Wal-Mart has 3 levels, Sears has 12. It's obvious which works better. But determining the number of levels is based on several variables, of which time to action is crucial. In addition, as Elliott Jaques points out in *Requisite Organization,* the cognitive capability of the people and how they are distributed through the different levels of an organization is of paramount importance.

Yes, there need to be levels, but we must structure them according to the caveats of *complexity* (of the work to be done), *competency* (of the people doing the work), and *time to action* (dissolving the problem). In a world of blinding speed, an organization must respond quickly and effectively, and it can't be done under the antiquated umbrella of span of control. When time is the focus, it drives the need for cross-functional thinking and action, from the top to the bottom of the organization, and from this come speed and flexibility, and people working on the job that's not being done. It eliminates white space and waste.

Companies that can create time to action context can collapse production times from 14 weeks to three weeks, or from six months to one month. Time to action is imperative. McDonald's knows it. Levi Strauss knows it. ABB knows it. Caterpillar knows it. Hallmark knows it. Chrysler knows it. IBM is learning it. Kodak is trying to learn it. General Motors is struggling to learn it. And many, many more have yet to learn.

Allowment (Puts Point of Authority Where It Belongs)

Empowering of employees without ensuring that they are first entitled (that they have information, skills, and authority) is like sending soldiers into rough terrain with no maps, supplying them with weapons but no ammunition, and providing no specialized training. It's a doomed mission. However, if we can see the context in which the soldiers operate differently, then we can expect much different results. The new context is one in which we *allow* the soldiers to decide and do whatever is required to complete a successful mission.

The success of the mission is directly tied to their well-being, as well as to the ongoing forward progress of the overall organization. First, the direction, objectives, and priorities are clear. Then, the troops must become entitled (capable) to take on the mission. To reach entitlement, they can take more training, access more information, request more resources, and make all decisions (they have the authority).

This new context not only allows them to fully engage the assignment, it also gives them the flexibility, speed, and motivation to meet conflict and do whatever has to be done to deliver the needed results. It's quite different thinking than that created by the sacrament of empowerment, where *entitlement before allowment doesn't happen.* For example, the famous Navy Seals are superbly trained, and one of the important parts of their training is the establishment of a set of values that allows each member of a team to make decisions without any communications. The Seals have a value system, information, skills, and authority on which they can act in complete alignment with other members and the overall values of the team—if necessary, without ever communicating directly. This always allows them to know when to move forward, retreat, abort, or change.

Allowment is not simply a semantic change. First and foremost, it's about understanding the new context—one in which employees are allowed to take on the information, skills, and authority they need, allowed to understand where to move in the organization, and allowed to be accountable for results. Obviously, they are not allowed until they are entitled, then the point of authority can shift to the point of occurrence, and they can do whatever they have to do to achieve the objectives.

Old thoughtware won't relinquish authority because it thinks authority assigns control. Wrong! As control spreads outward—with the expansion of information and knowledge—authority and entitlement must be there. If they aren't, organizational change will fall apart wherever the point of authority is located. The counter-mistake is empowerment, whereby those currently in authority move authority downline before the new decision makers are entitled—before they have the information, skills, and authority—regardless of their inherent capability.

In today's organization we must move to allowment and wean ourselves from delegating authority and fostering the old thoughtware that someone can empower someone else. Allowment confers on the individual the right to make decisions without higher approval, have the authority to assemble the required resources, and accept accountability. It's about decision making at the point of variance (where the problem is). This fundamental change in thinking significantly increases the organization's flexibility and resilience to change, while decreasing the resistance to change.

• GREETINGS—TO YOUR OWN DECISION MAKING •
When customers actually decide, design, and manufacture your product you've pushed the point of variance well down the line. This type of new thinking is behind the "make your own greeting card" machines. With these machines, customers are given the information and capability (thanks to technology) to write and design their own card on the spot, as they want it, when they want it. Great value, great flexibility, great responsiveness!

Notes

1. "What's New at GM? Cars, for a Change," *The New York Times,* September 8, 1996, pp. 3–10.

2. Charles M. Savage, *Fifth Generation Management* (Boston: Butterworth-Heineman, 1990).

Knowledge of the Whole   6

Perplexity is the beginning of knowledge.

—Kahlil Gibran

Leaving old context behind can be a harrowing experience. It's not like leaving home and going to the office. It's more like leaving home knowing you'll never return but not knowing exactly where you're going. That's what moving from the old thoughtware of division of labor to the new thoughtware of knowledge is all about: It's a major contextual shift. Most companies—and the people in them—fear the new context of knowledge, not because it's a bad idea but because of the perceived difficulty of moving from the comfort of current silos to the unknown of shared knowledge. It's downright scary. It's not the new context that threatens us; it's the process of changing to it. So we stay stuck in old thoughtware because we don't know how to rid ourselves of it. Let's get rid of it once and for all.

Divided We Fall

In the post-industrial era, the success of a corporation lies more in its intellectual and systems capabilities than in its physical assets ... but surprisingly little attention has been given to managing professional intellect.[1]

Look around the organization. So much is designed around the old division of labor thoughtware. Look at the hierarchy: vice presidents of every specialty you can imagine, assistant vice presidents, assistants to the assistants, supervisors of supervisors, skilled workers, semi-skilled workers, and non-skilled workers (downsizing and delayering have gotten rid of people, but not the non-value added activity, the redundancy that is the waste). All of these function according to their individual roles, all in deep troughs slicing through the organization. The thinking and theme are consistent: *Divided we shall conquer.* In this scenario of departmentalization, there's little coming together of the collective knowledge of the organization. Why? Competition. As Hout and Carter put it, "Besides holding divergent views of the business, top level managers also have real conflicts of interest. However much they may need to cooperate, they also compete with one another—for resources, for recognition, and ultimately the top job."[2]

Even in the attempts at process-complete departments, performance hasn't improved because although the management of the process changed, the context in which everyone worked did not. Many mind-sets remain set in the old thoughtware. In breaking the mind-set, Majchrzak and Wang posit that "something that is often overlooked is the tendency of managers and reengineering teams to underestimate the actions required to transform the way employees behave and work with one another. They assume that simply changing their organizational structures from functional units into process-complete departments will cause people to shed their functional mind-sets."[3] Majchrzak and Wang's three-year study (1994–1996) of U.S. electronics manufacturers proved this assumption wrong.

Look at the structure: top ranking department heads lined up, office after office, in some predetermined pecking order that reflects power, stature, fiefdom, and *assumed* importance to the organization. Process and structure can be changed, but it doesn't change this inbred divisive thinking. At Kodak, for example, the manufacturing department was far more important than the service department—which they sold a big part of in 1996. At General Motors, the engineering department is more important than sales. And at Citibank, finance sure as heck comes before marketing. But history has shown where these organizations have had many of their problems. Once again, why? Division of labor.

Look at cross-functionality (or lack of it). If cross-functionality isn't universal, from top to bottom, in both form and thought, then it's a false idol. It can't work. When cross-functional teams—no matter how well-intended—have their final accountability resting somewhere above them in a functional role (i.e., a vice-president), then their effect is limited. Similarly, when there is cross-functionality but no expulsion of old thoughtware, then nothing sustainable happens. Look at our compensation and reward systems: pay for utilization (e.g., piecework), reward cost reduction while ignoring growth (e.g., downsizing), bonus short-term profits and share value in lieu of long-term growth (check out CEOs' compensation packages these days), recognize and reward departmental performance (e.g., engineering excellence versus time-to-market or vice-versa), pay employees as if they were commodities in a demand–supply equation. It's a dog's breakfast that has no relationship to the organization's critical ingredient: *knowledge*. It is reward for isolated results and for part's performance, when it should be for knowledge.

United We Stand

Successful companies in the 21st century will be those who do the best job of capturing, storing, and leveraging what their employees know.
— LEWIS E. PLATT, CHAIRMAN, HEWLETT-PACKARD

Division of labor stands tall against wave after wave of programs and teams trying earnestly to overcome the barriers to change. It divides knowledge and conquers nothing. On the other hand, knowledge of the whole brings individuals and their knowledge together in a common effort and conquers all. Knowledge of the whole, interchangeable skills based on shared knowledge, and focus on the total process, not the parts, develops a universally cross-functional approach that creates significant competitive advantage. Knowledge thrusts through divisions, makes isolated functions obsolete, carves up traditional thinking, and in its wake gives birth to new process thinking.

• The Great (or Not So Great) Canoe Race •

The great canoe race was legendary in Middletown. It pitted the top two companies in the county in a head-to-head series of races in quest of the cherished title, "Organization Excellence." It was more than a battle of the fittest, it was a battle of skill and wits.

Each company had arrived in the finals through a series of elimination races with competitors in their respective classes and the final was a best-of-seven series that took place over two weeks.

Surprisingly, this year the defending champion, Conglomerate, Inc., was up against a new and much smaller company, Nawledge, Inc. In years past, the final two competitors were usually Middletown's biggest companies, Conglomerate, Inc., and Titan, Inc.

The whole town turned out on the banks of the Processippi River for the opening contest. Conglomerate was manning a huge war canoe with 12 burly paddlers and two steerpersons—a woman from engineering sat fore and a man from finance sat aft. Conglomerate had won this race many times before and the only change from last year's plan was the addition of the woman from engineering. The paddlers were all well-deployed specialists: The sprint paddlers, with their light, shallow dipping paddles, occupied alternating positions, evenly dispersed along each side. Sitting directly behind the sprint paddlers were four long-paddlers, with their deep, wide-blade paddles geared for long distance endurance. Behind them, two on each side, were the change-of-direction paddlers, with their special left or right steering paddles. It was a formidable team—all highly trained specialists with lots of experience. Just before entering the water they raised a bright red and white banner to a cheering crowd. It read, "One for all and all for one."

Beside them was the team from Nawledge, Inc. The contrast was stark. They were entering a much smaller craft that carried only eight paddlers, even though each team was allowed to consist of 12 people. The canoe was about two-thirds the length of Conglomerate's war canoe and it looked much lighter. All eight members of the team were paddlers—there were no specialized steering people—and each carried three different paddles. As they climbed into their canoe, everyone noticed that there were four other team members, but they remained on shore. This was strange.

The starting gun boomed and the competitors dug deep. Thousands watched. The speed of the four sprint paddlers, plus the power of the four long paddlers, plus the effort of the four steering paddlers gave Conglomerate an early margin over the eight Nawledge paddlers. On shore the CEO of Conglomerate smiled with satisfaction. He knew his people had done this many times before. Also on shore, the other four members of the Nawledge team began to jog along the riverbank, parallel with their canoe. As they ran past the Conglomerate CEO he shrugged and laughed, "What do they know?"

Soon the picture changed. All eight of the Nawledge paddlers took in their sprint paddles and brought out their long-distance paddles. Eight deep-dipping paddles quickly pushed their canoe past Conglomerate. The Conglomerate crew looked surprised. The fore steerperson called for more sprint paddling. The aft steerperson called for stronger long paddling, and the steering paddlers stopped, awaiting new instructions. They didn't know what to do next. As they neared a sharp and treacherous bend in the river, the fore steerperson called for hard-to-port steering by the steering paddlers. The long paddlers stopped while the sprint paddlers increased their effort. The big war canoe pointed to port and began to navigate the turn.

Meanwhile, the Nawledge crew exchanged all but two of their paddles for steering paddles and made a sharp and decisive turn to port, quickly changed back to sprint paddles, and shot past their competitor. Then they changed again to eight long paddles and opened up a sizeable lead. All the time, their on-shore members were running in parallel. Behind now, Conglomerate steerpersons were encouraging the four long paddlers to dig deep to try to close the gap. The Conglomerate CEO wasn't worried as he received reports from his downstream people. Soon they would be approaching the rapids and the superiority of their steering paddlers, plus their much heavier and more durable canoe, would give them a major advantage. They had planned on this—they knew the rapids were a real test—so they had engineered and built the canoe and trained the crew for it. Any time lost on the upper portion of the river would be regained through the rapids. Their superior strength would allow them to blast right through while the competitor's lighter craft could easily capsize or be damaged by rocks.

By the time Nawledge reached the top of the rapids, they had a five- to six-minute lead. Suddenly, all eight paddlers switched again to the steering paddles and took the canoe directly ashore. There, two of the onshore members hoisted the lightweight craft over their shoulders and broke into a run. In step right behind them was the rest of the team. A few minutes later, two other fresh, onshore members took over carrying the canoe. In less than five minutes the Nawledge team arrived at the bottom of the rapids and reentered their canoe. The two original shore members took over in the canoe and two others took over on shore.

Meanwhile, at the top of the rapids, Conglomerate braced for the turbulence of the rising, white water. Steerpersons yelled often-conflicting instructions, sprinters held on, long paddlers held on, and steering paddlers poised for action. Two and a half minutes of constant upheaval, considerable confusion, disparate effort, hard knocks, and disgruntled mumblings brought Conglomerate twisting and twirling out of the final eddy—just in time to see Nawledge disappearing around a distant bend in the river.

Suddenly, Conglomerate's new fore steerperson (the engineer) decided to make changes. She would reconfigure the crew and change the roles and positions of the paddlers. Put the steerers up front, group all the long paddlers together at the back, and get the sprinters in the middle. Or get the sprinters to do long paddling (even with their shallow paddles) and the steerers to do the sprinting. In this way, they could get more power for the long, flat course that lay ahead. The only problem was, the paddlers couldn't, or didn't want to, move. They were not comfortable with moving from one side to the other or changing roles. And the aft steerperson (the accountant) disagreed because of the cost associated with all these changes. Meanwhile, the downstream reports going back up top to the CEO indicated chaos was at hand. *He* had to make a decision and get the ship moving again, and there was no time to call in consultants. The message came down loud and clear: Quickly reconfigure, apply the new rapid paddling program and then dig deeper to generate more output. Superior power would endure.

As the teams encountered more rapids, portages, and constant turbulence, the knowledge, flexibility, and maneuverability of the Nawledge team proved unbeatable. They won the first race hands down. In the second race, Conglomerate added more long paddlers and reduced the steering paddlers. They overturned in the rapids. For the third race, they kept the steerers and reduced the sprinters. They were 10 minutes behind at the top of the first rapids. In the fourth race, they disposed of the steerperson and added two sprinters. They ran aground just below the rapids. They lost in four straight races.

For next year, rumor has it that Conglomerate is re-engineering its canoe, downsizing crew, recruiting more specialized crew, and providing much more training for each position. The Nawledge crew is apparently doing more cross-training, gathering new knowledge about the river and surrounding terrain, exchanging information among specialists, and waiting until the very last minute to design and build their canoe.

The antidote for division of labor disease is shared knowledge through cross-functionality, but history has shown that a heavy dose of cross-functional teams is no sure cure. In fact, the wisdom of teams has been under question for some time. Teams have no doubt been helpful—in fueling enthusiasm, improving communications, and making changes, for instance—but their contribution has been limited and at times counterproductive, because the cross-functionality operates within an unchanged context. *The cross-functionality has not been universal* and it has not addressed the underlying thought-ware, so functional thinking persists. Although teams reign, functionality continues to rule. Senior management, in spite of good intentions and oratorical lip service, do not practice what they preach. Thousands of cross-functional teams have run up against a glass ceiling and have only been mere content change within old context. When a cross-functional team reports to a functional head who is accountable for final outcome, nothing of any magnitude changes. It must be a *cross-functional head* (someone with, or access to, all the knowledge) who has final accountability.

Getting to Process Thinking and Universal Cross-Functionality

The wellspring of new knowledge in the organization comes from process thinking, not functional thinking. There is no shortage of knowledge; it abounds within the organization. But it is compartmentalized, boxed up, and trapped in a thousand different thoughts.

> *If two heads are better than one, what is the value of the collective knowledge of a hundred heads? Or a thousand? Or, for that matter, an entire enterprise?*
> —BOWLES & HAMMOND, ASQC

The first step to installing new thoughtware is to *unlock the knowledge,* to open up the doors to *universal cross-functionality.* To have universal cross-functionality there must be knowledge of the whole process, across the whole spectrum, and a large dose of new thinking. The old thoughtware must go, for it is cross-functionality's worst enemy. There can be no division, no cross-purposes, no misunderstanding, no isolated functional thinking. Cross-functionality must be ubiquitous, top to bottom, and embody new thoughtware. When it is, it disrupts the status quo, shatters the glass ceiling, opens up fault lines of mammoth opportunity, and ignites contextual shift.

That's the idea: Bring together, through universal cross-functionality, all the knowledge needed to understand the entire business process, generate new thinking, and install new thoughtware on which to operate. In parallel, create an environment that allows people to be constantly on intimate terms with the required knowledge. Make new thinking an ingrained habit. Only then do we have a chance of managing the business *for* the future, instead of *from* the past.

Senior (across the very top) cross-functionality is the bedrock for cohesive and integrated knowledge. Bear in mind that this coming together is *not* a programmatic attempt at consensus—that's old thoughtware, and never in the history of business has consensus effectively replaced leadership. Conversely, leadership without knowledge of the whole process—and an awareness of the debilitating limitations of old thoughtware—is just as useless. *Universal cross-functionality is a prerequisite of leadership because it develops an understanding of the whole and a recognition of old thoughtware, thereby allowing for the expulsion of old thoughtware, the setting of clear direction, and the provision of a platform for contextual shift.*

> *Leadership is the accountability for getting others to move in the same direction.*
>
> —Dr. Elliott Jaques

The absence of shared knowledge and the lack of understanding of the process as a whole can be seen in simple, everyday comments like the following:

Sales: "Why don't we build what we're selling?
Manufacturing: "Why don't we sell what's in inventory?"

———

Customer Service: "What happens to an order after you're done with it?"
Order Entry: "I don't know."

———

Purchasing: "Do you know how much those double-stress cables cost?"
Engineering: "No, why?"

Such common conflicts are only overcome when knowledge of the whole can be accessed and collated—anytime, anywhere—across the organization. The employees of Microsoft can do it. They have the collective knowledge, cross-functional access to that knowledge, a clear understanding of purpose, specific targets, the required skills, and the capability (a process) to change at will—and in a nanosecond.

Knowledge of the whole requires a new configuration that interlocks knowledge and allows for smooth, integrated processes that respond to a centralized focus on the customer. One company's reconfigured approach is represented in Figure 6-1. With the customer's needs at the center, the entire organization's knowledge and information exchange revolves around this focus, and drives the major components of the company.

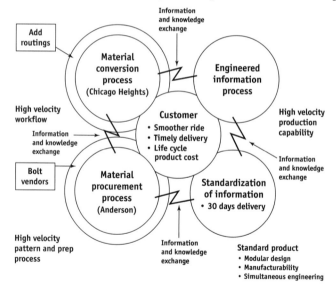

Figure 6-1. Reconfigured Approach for a Customer Focus

Later, we will talk about the importance of senior management's role in setting out the business's case for action (an operationalized statement of direction, objectives, tasks, and measures). Knowledge is a cornerstone of this case for action; therefore one of senior management's first steps must be to amass the needed knowledge through universal cross-functionality. Management cannot articulate a case for action until they do. So create that senior cross-functional team (with no division of labor) and start by injecting some new thoughtware. Remember, there's been many a senior cross-functional team that has failed abysmally because they changed the structure without changing the thinking—especially their own. This isn't more of the same old cross-functionality, using the same old tools; this is about a new structure *and* new thinking. It's very different.

Does This Mean No Specialization?

Not at all. No doubt specialization is important. After all, we can't have general practitioners doing brain surgery or metallurgists selling widgets. But all their knowledge and specialization must come together. Usually, the value of specialists is greatly diminished because their specialization, their piece of the process, is isolated somewhere in a falsely fabricated, division of labor silo or in their mind-set (even if they are part of a process-complete team/department). A good case in point is Honda during its down years when design engineering became too diverted by its own goals and produced cars that were too hard to build, cost too much, and didn't click with buyers. So engineering was pushed out of the driver's seat. CEO Kawamoto wasn't ignoring engineering; rather, he was harnessing it to the rest of the company.[4] The rest is history. Isolated specialization, such as that which Kawamoto stopped, means that time and cost of development is dinosauric, and it prohibits companies from responding quickly and effectively. They are regularly beaten to, and in, the marketplace.

We need to see and place specialization in context, the new context of knowledge, whereby all the knowledge can be rapidly absorbed in order to deliver immediate response. It can't be done over barriers, under divisional doors, or through closed minds. The sharing of knowledge "is critical because intellectual assets, unlike physical assets, increase in value with use. Properly stimulated, knowledge and intellect grow exponentially when shared."[5] However, just bringing specialists together through cross-functionality won't necessarily do it. Start with jettisoning old thoughtware in order to generate new thinking. Then, reconfigure and disperse the resources. Pull the metallurgist out of the department, place him on the New Product Introduction Team (or other complete-process teams), and get his specialty—his knowledge—into play. But don't stop there. Give him new thoughtware that allows him to help change the context in which he works.

Nowhere is the power of knowledge better understood than in technology companies (witness Silicon Valley). They understand, operate, and think in the context of speed and constant change, and total access to all the required knowledge. They never "grew up" in any other type of context, so they don't think with old thoughtware. Unfortunately, most of our organizations did grow up in the old context and cannot break out of it. Business in the (new) technology context is a good example of the scientific theory of chaos: There is seeming chaos and no apparent control, yet definitive patterns exist. Growth, movement, and a greater purpose are understood and achieved, not in spite of, but because of, the chaos—constantly forming, deforming, banding, and dis-banding—in response to what must be done. They live the virtual organization, bringing resources together to meet daily changing priorities, then reallocating those same resources when the task is accomplished or the priorities change.

This last point is important. How many teams—good, well-intentioned teams—continue to persevere long after the particular task they're working on has ceased to be a priority? Too many. Teams cannot be fixed assets, eternal machines, designed to run until the run is finished. If there's a new race tomorrow, they must be capable of switching horses and competing anew. They must be as quick to disperse as they are to form. What must happen is the interchange of knowledge to wherever it is needed most. In all of this, knowledge is the linchpin. So how do we craft the linchpin?

New Thoughtware Generates New Knowledge

Knowledge is a product, perhaps our most important product. Our companies can no longer focus on simply building widgets, or appliances, VCRs, chemicals, food, or toothpaste. We must focus on building knowledge—the most critical ingredient in creating all the others.

In the industrial era we converted material into product, now we must convert knowledge into products and services.
— PETER DRUCKER

In industrial times the basics of economics were driven by scarcity—scarcity of resources, scarcity of products, or scarcity of demand. Today, in the knowledge economy, we have a new set of rules based on abundance, not scarcity. There is an abundance of knowledge, and it grows exponentially. The challenge, therefore, is to capture and utilize the knowledge. It takes learning. Not yesterday's learning, but tomorrow's learning. Learning that understands tomorrow. Learning that requires new thoughtware.

Knowledge is a product of learning, and how we learn or acquire knowledge is crucial to how we grow. Much has been written about learning, but there is always more to learn. There is little disagreement on its importance; however, there are as many techniques as there are teachers, and the best platform on which to start is experience.

Shared experience is shared knowledge, and the simple act of bringing people together to exchange experience and knowledge generates extensive new knowledge. Connect the people, get them in the same rooms, in the same groups, on the same networks (with a common purpose and process), and watch the knowledge build. It's like a hidden power within that only needs exposure to flourish. It initiates a process of germination and cross-pollination. The learning spreads like lightning across a summer sky. Knowledge jumps from person to person while awareness and understanding mounts. Real dialogue. Real communication. Realization of the importance of the whole and the value of linking all the parts. Then inject new thoughtware and the learning compounds. The value of knowledge grows exponentially.

First we need a critical mass of people who understand the power of knowledge and can build a process of learning—on a platform of new thoughtware—that continuously generates new knowledge. Take AMP, for example. A $5 billion world leader in the manufacture of electronic/electrical interconnection devices, AMP is a knowledge-rich company which recognizes the value of knowledge. "The commitment and ability to develop and share valuable knowledge—both with our customers and our 40,000 people around the world—is a key enabler of AMP's success," says Paul A. Timashenka, divisional vice-president.[6]

Live the Experience

Tell me and I'll probably forget.
Show me and I may remember.
Let me do it, and I'll never forget.

Only 4 percent of what we learn comes from a classroom.[7] The real power of learning is in the *doing*. Learning is a social exchange among people. Understanding how we learn has far-reaching implications to how we manage and how we try to build and maximize the collective knowledge in the organization. Learning is a subject requiring far more in-depth discussion than we can give it here, but the fundamentals of experiential and group learning directly apply to the issue of installing new knowledge thoughtware.

Experience is a great teacher, but she has her price. Mistakes can kill'ya, and the time it takes to learn on the job can be an enormous sunken cost. Also, it's not just a matter of acquiring new knowledge; it's a matter of developing new thinking, which in real time seems to take forever. The alternative is simulation—not simply simulation of general business practices and principles, but simulation of *your* business, *your* issues, *your* thoughtware.

Contextual Simulation

Many of us already know and understand the basic principles of change management and the practices of restructuring, redesign, reengineering, quality assurance, cycle time reduction, and so on; however, few of us have gone through the proverbial knothole of *rethinking the very context in which we do business,* whereby we experience a comprehensive sharing of knowledge in pursuit of new thinking and new context. Simulation is often used, but too many times it doesn't bite because it is *not* addressing contextual change, it's only playing with content.

Contextual simulation radically shifts thinking. It allows everyone to see, hear, touch, and do what can't be done any other way. It works with a group, creates a socio-business environment, locks out fear and risk, and allows for the discovery of everything from *what you don't know* to *what you can do.* It annihilates old thoughtware and lets knowledge of the whole germinate new thoughtware. Contextual simulation is refreshingly wrenching, and like many good antidotes, quick and relatively painless.

At a $100 million manufacturing company in the Midwest, the installation of new thoughtware exposed a wealth of new knowledge and created a significant contextual shift—not to mention freeing up 30–35 percent more capacity. Initially, the issue was one of generating more cash. Due to a recent buyout, the company had debt to retire, so they planned to take all the traditional steps to cut costs and increase sales in order to generate much needed cash. This was their plan, that is, until they simulated new thoughtware in a new context. The simulated experience sent them after the invisible capital asset of time. By collapsing time, they released significant working capital, and the extra capacity and cash was generated without any expansion of bricks, mortar, or machines. The process allowed everyone to collectively share knowledge of the whole, address the greater context instead of the specific problem, blow up old thoughtware, experience the outcomes of new thought-ware, see where the opportunities were, eliminate the waste, and release the hidden cash—millions in working capital.

Contextual simulation using new thoughtware creates the learning and knowledge that can be translated into the real environment—and it can be done in a matter of days:

- *Round one:* Exposes *what you don't know* (the cornerstone of new thoughtware). You see complexity, lack of communications, and old thoughtware for the primary impediments they are, and where they are. It creates and measures your baseline—where you are today.
- *Round two:* Demonstrates that you *can* do better with an expo-sure to opportunities, an expulsion of old thoughtware, and measurement of improvements—all the time still using the same resources, but with more knowledge and better use of them. Some incremental gains are made.
- *Round three:* Installs a process that engages new thoughtware and changes the context. It captures the non-traditional measures, generates new knowledge, and accesses the opportunities. It allows you to break through and reach never-before-expected objectives.
- *Outcomes:* Generates a major contextual shift, delivers veneer-ripping learning, creates new knowledge, and exposes the enormous potential for change.
- *And:* This whole simulated process can be readily transferred into the real environment.

Humpty Dumpty Could Have Been
Saved Through Simulation

All the king's horses and all the king's men could have put Humpty Dumpty together again—if they'd used thoughtware simulation. Simulation can break current thinking without cracking the whole basket of eggs, so to speak. You can experience the fall without taking the leap. Simulation of new thoughtware coalesces newfound knowledge, dissects process, shatters old assumptions, and then puts it all together again.

One of the early breakthroughs out of old thoughtware can be done with a piece of new thoughtware that changes what is normally thought of as fixed, a given, to variable.

• ELECTRIFIED THINKING •

In the case of the manufacturer of electrical motors, it was a question of how good could they be in converting prototypes to new sales when they were already the best in the business, with a 27 percent conversion rate.

Q: "So how does 27 percent conversion compare?"
A: "It's darn good."

Q: "Is it good enough?"
A: "Sure! We're beating the competition regularly."

Q: "How much better could you be?"
A: "Oh, we could do 30 percent if we stood on our head, but we don't have to."

Q: "Why not 50 percent? Or 60 percent?"
A: "Not possible."

Q: "Why not?"

A: "We're the best because we have the best quality and price, and we can deliver in 10 weeks. We can't do any better on quality and price. They're already the best."

Q: "What if the competition matches you on quality and price?"

A: "Well, we'll just have to get better."

Q: "What if you got quicker? Compete on time? Would it make a difference?"

A: "Uh, maybe."

Q: "What if you could deliver in 10 days instead of 10 weeks? Do you think it would make a difference?"

A: Sure, but 10 days is impossible."

Q: "Why?"

A: "Too many steps. Too many delays, changes. It takes more than 10 days just to do the blueprints. Even after the blueprints are done, the customer usually sits on them, then changes go back and forth, then we wait for an opening on a production line. It takes time...."

Q: "What if an engineer goes to the customer with blueprints, reviews and changes them, and gets approval all in one step?"

A: "Nice idea, but not practical. We've got customers all over the country, plus overseas. It would cost an enormous amount in travel and time. We can't have engineers flying all over the place."

Q: "What would the value be in converting 40 percent of all prototypes?"

A: "Oh (takes out a calculator) ... about $30 million a year."

Q: "That covers a lot of travel expenses, don't you think?"

A: "Yeah, but that's only part of the problem. Then we have to get the blueprints back to manufacturing and make manufacturing drawings."

Q: "You have a CAD/CAM system, don't you?"

A: "Yeah, but it's local."

Q: "What if we arm our engineers with laptops, punch the drawings back into the CAD system, download into the CAM, onto the CNC machines?"

A: Uh ... yeah, but now you're talking big money and...."

Q: "Don't focus on the money, focus on the time factor. Remember, time is the resource and money the metric. How long would it take if you could download?"

A: "If you think of it in those terms, I suppose we could do it in less than 10 weeks."

Q: "Let's simulate it."

In this story (a true one), time became the competitive variable, and in spite of the assumptions that it couldn't be done and that it would cost too much, the thinking changed, and the story has a better-than-Hollywood ending. The company achieved a never-before-thought-of conversion rate of 72 percent on prototypes and increased annual sales by more than $60 million.

Take any story, take any problem (whether it be distribution, supply, marketing, engineering, or manufacturing), and the required process for getting to new context is the same. If it's an issue of division of labor and division of thinking, then we must move to new knowledge and new thoughtware to create new context. Gather the collective knowledge, disperse the clouds of risk and fear, make the heretofore immovable assumptions variables, simulate *your* business, and most importantly, inject new thoughtware, from whence will come new context.

• BOLTED DOWN THINKING •

Long after the first iron horse headed west across the Mississippi, we are still building and maintaining an enormous network of railroads; and if you're in the business of designing, manufacturing, and distributing railworks material, every nut, bolt, and tie counts. Standards, specs, and costs are paramount. Or so the thinking goes. There is a wide variety in the size of bolts used, and it's not an insignificant cost in terms of the time it takes to spec, make, inventory, assemble, and distribute them.

Q: "Why don't we put the same bolt in every rail?"
A: "Oh man, that can't be done. Every railroad has its own standards, and there's a lot of them."

Q: "What if you could get them to agree on having the same standard?"
A: "Never happen."

Q: "What do they buy on?"
A: "Price."

Q: "What if we offered them a 20 percent price reduction if they changed their standard to be the same as others, while still meeting all their other specs?"
A: "They'd never agree."

Q: "What if we offered a 30 percent reduction in price?"
A: "They wouldn't agree."

Q: "What if we gave it to them for free?"
A: "Okay ... yeah, they might go for it. But we'd never give bolts away."

Q: "Of course not, but there is *some* point where they would agree to a common standard, right?"

A: "Yeah, probably. But not everyone would settle for a number six bolt. Some want number eights and we can't be giving number eights to everybody who wants sixes."

Q: "Why not?"

A: "It costs more for eights. We'd be losing money if we substituted eights for sixes."

Q: "How long is the setup time in changing over from eights to sixes."

A: "I don't know, but somebody in manufacturing would know."

Q: "And what's the cost of maintaining separate inventories, sales and accounting records, and changeovers in assembly for two different types of bolts?"

A: "Quite a bit I guess. Somebody else might know."

Q: "Maybe more than the cost of giving everybody number eights?"

A: "Maybe...."

The knowledge was brought together, the thinking changed, and costs collapsed significantly. The savings from standardizing specs on numerous items and providing number eight bolts in all material was very significant.

Knowledge: A Product and a Real Catalyst

The issue of knowledge is so important, and yet so underestimated and overlooked. Oh, we all talk about it, but few do much beyond talk. This can't continue if the organization is to grow. Knowledge is a critical footing for the installation of new thoughtware in any organization. At first it's threatening (that's why it's so often given perfunctory attention), then disruptive, then it becomes provocative, then challenging, and then a true agent of change. We must grab hold of this most critical component of change and start with new, experiential learning at the most senior levels, install new thoughtware, and create the most powerful knowledge product possible. Learning and the development of new knowledge must become a part of every person's accountability.

Notes

[1] James Quinn, Philip Anderson, and Sydney Finkelstein, "Managing Professional Intellect: Making the Most of the Best," *Harvard Business Review,* March–April 1996, p. 71.

[2] Thomas Hout and John Carter, "Getting It Done: New Roles for Executives," *Harvard Business Review,* November–December 1995, p. 135.

[3] Ann Majchrzak and Qianwei Wang, "Breaking the Functional Mind-set in Process Organizations," *Harvard Business Review,* September–October 1996, p. 93.

[4] "On Track," *Fortune,* September 9, 1996, p. 4.

[5] Quinn, Anderson, Finkelstein, "Managing Professional Intellect: Making the Most of the Best," p. 75.

[6] Jerry Bowles and Josh Hammond, "Competing on Knowledge," *Fortune,* September 9, 1996, p. 7.

[7] Michael Lombardo and Robert Eichinger, *Career Architect Manual* (Greensboro, NC: Executive Studies by the Center for Creative Leadership, Lominger Limited, Inc.).

Measurement of What Matters | 7

The central act of the coming era is to
connect everything to everything.

—KEVIN KELLY

"All our departments have goals and measurements." Bzzzz—wrong answer! But don't be discouraged. Most organizations have the wrong answer, and besides, it's not the answer that matters, it's having the right question. And the right question goes something like this:

"Does your organization collectively have a measurement system that acts as a master navigational system in which *you* build specific objectives and align all information, measure true performance drivers, integrate all measures, provide easy access, generate continual feedback, and deliver all measures in a language of the employee's choice that results in a common scorecard for all?"

That is the question. And seldom is the answer a simple yes or no.

History has given us a plethora of measurements and an endless mountain of information, most of it on paper, and yet it has never given us what we really need: complete integration and clarity in results, roles, communications, decision making, accountability, focus, direction, and overall performance. The majority of current measurement systems can't deliver what we need, and the dissatisfaction with the information is widespread.

Most of our measuring is evaluative. It starts with financials and covers many operational measures, but it primarily measures how we do rather than providing navigational information that can tell us where we are, the direction in which to head, speed and performance required, and how to deliver all of these in real time. We traditionally measure the organization's value; however, calculating the organization's value with such tools as balance sheets, profit and loss statements, cash flow statements, economic value added (EVA), leveraged value added (LVA), and market value added (MVA) does not give management an understanding of *how* to increase value. That's because these are not navigational tools.

Most of the measures we have might be reassuring, but they're desperately lacking. They're based on thinking that has evolved from 14th century double-entry bookkeeping and early 19th century standard costing, through to the more recent measurements of ISO 9000, activity-based accounting, intellectual capital, and EVA/MVA/LVA (see Figure 7-1). These methods are "me-assuring," but they are not measuring much of significant value. The problem is that in large part they're all financially based concepts. We're still measuring what's easy and that which tells us that what we have done is okay, instead of measuring what we need to know to help us create the future.

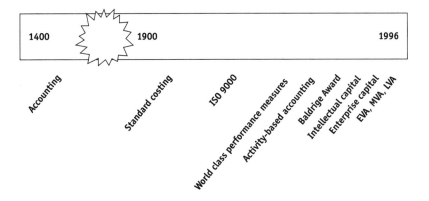

Figure 7-1. The Emergence of a New Way to Measure

As a case in point, traditionally we have measured the number of bolts in inventory or on the floor as an expense item; if we are to focus on measuring what matters, however, we should measure the time consumed as a result of the bolts. Even though the bolts are a measurement on the profit and loss statement, they really are more important as a factor in process flow. But because it's difficult to measure bolts as a flow item, we ignore such measurement and simply measure them as an expense on the P&L. "In a knowledge-based company," says Judy Lewent, the highly regarded chief financial officer of Mereck & Co., "the accounting system doesn't capture anything, really."[1]

Measurement and Motivation: The Pyramid of Relevance

Traditional measurements such as return on investment, return on net assets, and return on equity have little relevance to most of the people who are responsible for actually producing the results. The things that are relevant to them—the real drivers of performance—are not measured. For example, under customer satisfaction certain specific measures can be made quite relevant to those employees handling specific tasks like customer complaints, shipping accuracy, and invoicing accuracy. Measurements must be relevant to everyone and available in every corner of the organization.

A measurement system that takes *cascading relevance* into account and is designed to link all components can produce real motivation and measurable action. Such a measurement system, developed by Cross and Lynch, is shown in Figure 7-2. This pyramid depicts the relevance of issues and measures from the top to the bottom of an organization. At the top of the pyramid is the vision. Directly below the vision are the internal and external factors that are crucial to the whole organization—such as market share, competitive positioning, and strategic alliances on the external side, and return on net assets, return on investment, and earnings before taxes on the internal side. These factors are not particularly relevant on the front lines. Coming down another level, however, is the process view. At this level—customer satisfaction, flexibility, and productivity—the higher-level goals begin to be understood and applicable. Finally, at the lowest levels are the process drivers. These are the measurements that can be relevant to the people generating the results, the hands-on measurements that drive toward the top: quality, delivery, cycle time reduction, and waste or non-value-added ratios. Although not shown here, the process drivers break down even further into such things as setup time, number of parts in queue, rework, customer rejects, back orders, and so on. An organization must build this type of linkage in order to create the required relevance and performance outputs.

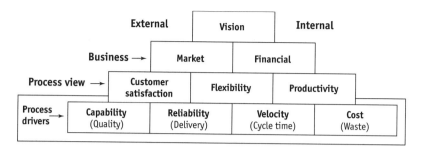

Figure 7-2. Pyramid of Relevant Measures

Hierarchy of Internal and External Measurement

Measurement must be in real time, at the point where it's needed when it's needed, and in meaningful language to the user; provide navigation as well as evaluation; engage rather than control; and be linked to all other measures. In order to accomplish this, there must be a clear picture available to everyone.

• IN YOUR FACE •

Coach Todd could not understand why his star basketball player, Ryan Leigh, was not performing up to his potential. The team was doing okay with an 8-2 record, but they were still averaging *less* than 75 points a game and their rebounding stunk. Ryan came out of high school as the most highly touted player in the state. With 26.7 points and 11.4 rebounds per game in his senior year, he was sought after by every major college in the country. He was Coach Todd's number one player, but so far this season he was averaging only 12.5 points and 5.7 rebounds, and now he was pressing. He knew he was a big factor in the offense and he was trying to carry the team, to help it get over the 75-points-per-game mark. Coach Todd had a thought.

"Ryan, instead of trying to score 30 points a game, grab all the rebounds, *and* set up everybody else, I want you to concentrate on a couple of things. You aren't measured on how many total points we score, or even if we win or lose. Your best measurements are points scored and rebounds. And you score the most when you attempt at least 9 or 10 three-point shots per game because you usually hit a third of them— that's 10 points right there. And, you should take at least another 15 shots from the field. You'll hit 50 percent—that's another 16 points. And with half a dozen free throw chances you're over 30 points every game. Don't worry about the other stuff. The rebounds will come automatically as a result of working to score more points.

They won the next game 91-84. Ryan scored 33 points and grabbed 9 rebounds. He liked the new measurements.

To change from easy to measure to what matters, we have to change the relevance *and* the context in which we measure. In other words, we have to change the thoughtware. Quinn, Anderson, and Finkelstein, in their *Harvard Business Review* article entitled "Managing Professional Intellect: Making the Most of the Best," suggest that companies should organize around intellect and "invert the organization," thereby "organizing themselves in patterns specifically tailored to the particular way their professional intellect creates value. Such organization often involves breaking away from traditional thinking about the role of the center as a directing force."[2] This is a changing context. Figure 7-3 shows this inverted hierarchy.

The authors cite NovaCare, the largest provider of rehabilitation care and one of the fastest growing healthcare companies in the United States, as one of many companies that have inverted their traditional organizational structure. "The former line hierarchy becomes a support structure and

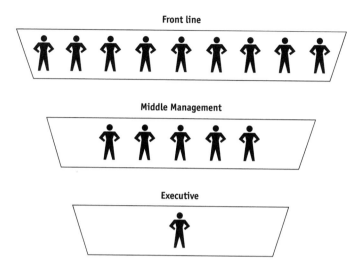

Figure 7-3. Inverted Hierarchy

the function of the former line managers changes: Instead of giving orders, they are now removing barriers, expediting resources, conducting studies, and acting as consultants. They support and help articulate the new culture."[3] It's a different context.

But they also point out that an inverted hierarchy doesn't always work. "A classic example is People Express, which consciously inverted its organization and enjoyed highly empowered and motivated point people, but lacked the systems or the computer infrastructure to enable them to adapt as the organization grew (they weren't entitled). They never changed the context. If such organizations fail, it is usually because—despite much rhetoric about inversion—their senior managers did not support the concept with thoroughly overhauled performance-measurement and reward systems."[4]

It's an Information Issue

It's all about the impact of information and what technology is doing with information. "Today, there are more than 100 million computers in the world, and computer companies predict that more than one billion will be in use by the turn of the century."[5] The primary purpose of computers, of course, is to manipulate information, and the total information available doubles every five years.[6] It is a deluge. A storm. A tidal wave. And somehow we have to corral the right information, transform it into performance measures, and allow it to give the organization the direction and motivation needed to get to the future.

> Twenty million "back-office" workers in the U.S.A process records and deliver messages or information for twenty three million managers and other professional knowledge workers (a 1.3/1 ratio).
>
> —U.S. Department of Labor Statistics

Dispense with Departmentalization

Step one: Get rid of departmentalization and all of its inherent measurements. This means crush departmentalized thinking. Thinking about and measuring the parts and keeping track of different pieces is a fast way to a slow death. It is not the parts that count or should be counted; it's the whole that matters, and *we have to be constantly in touch with both detailed and overall performance as it relates to the whole.*

This means using information to create unadulterated communications and instant response. In fact, it's more than a one-way information issue; rather, it's a two-way communication issue that must establish open, dynamic dialogue.

Remember: The aggregate of all relationships runs the organization, and two-way communication is the fodder and glue of relationships.

"No Communications" Is an Old Refrain

The number one complaint among employees is the lack of communication within an organization, and nowhere is its manifestation more obvious than with the issue of information. Communication will always be lacking if there is a lack of information about the whole business process. And regardless of how pervasive technology makes information, and no matter how wide the access, information remains a "fixed (as in frozen) asset" until it is transformed by thoughtware. Old thoughtware does a lousy job of transforming (unfreezing) information into good communication and making it a high, value-adding resource. An abundance of information with the same old measurement systems and continual efforts at improving communication achieves little if new thoughtware is not applied. New thoughtware transforms information and creates the communication needed in today's new context.

Today we have the means to break through these barriers because information is rampant and technology enables us to connect everything. All that's required is a measurement system that integrates and communicates it, thus providing real navigational support.

Navigation

Expert navigation is the only way to get there—to get anywhere, for that matter—and navigation without the right measurement is a course to disaster. The shoals and reefs of business failures are littered with organizations that had elaborate measurement and information systems but still had no idea where they were or where they were headed. One, two, or two dozen executives might have known where they wanted to go, but if the rest of the crew—the real drivers of the business—are down below in the dark, then trouble is inevitable.

As we said at the beginning of this chapter, navigation begins with information and measurement that describes where the organization is, where it's going, and how it's going to get there. Since Galileo's time, we've be able to establish position, direction, distance, and velocity, and yet, centuries later, in a time of exploding technology, we seldom apply this basic criteria to the proper navigation of our organizations. It isn't because of the lack of tools (surely technology has given us those); it's because of the wrong thoughtware. We're still trying to navigate with the wrong information, coming from departments, going into silos, and not being available where it's needed, when it's needed, in the form it's needed. So we drift like the Wreck of the Hesperus.

An Annealing Process

In the manufacturing of steel there is a process called annealing whereby the steel is put through a series of heating and cooling steps in order to align molecules in the same direction, thus increasing the strength of the steel. Annealing is also done to increase durability in plastics, enhance beauty in gemstones, and improve performance in semiconductors. Neil Larson, author of *Max Think* (1991), has borrowed and applied this term as it relates to organizations, and it is somewhat akin to what we need to accomplish with information and measurement in organizations. In determining what matters, the organization must refer its stated case for action (defined in Chapter 11), which sets out what success looks like. From this, the necessary knowledge, information, and measures are developed to describe the properties and attributes required for success. Then the information must be annealed, that is, aligned in accordance with the direction set forth in the case for action.

We cannot continue to measure discreet pieces of information and attempt to bring them together with departmentalized thinking, prescribe action, and expect to achieve some semblance of direction and continuity of performance (usually 50 percent of all objectives in an organization are in conflict). Instead, we must create an annealing process for information so that we begin to align all the measures in the business. This annealing arranges all relevant information and reflects the continuing status of the organization. What it does is describe the current state of any given attribute *and* what the desired state would be *if* it was to be aligned properly (the where you are and the where you want to be), and it's aligned with the overall direction, strategy, and goals of the organization. When all the information is annealed, the organization is much more capable of measuring position, direction, distance, and velocity. It is able, therefore, to navigate where it must go and change course in a moment's notice.

The first step is to identify those things that are *central to success,* those things that *need significant improvement,* and those things that *most accurately reflect performance of the total organization.* It's a list of crucial properties of the business and the corresponding attributes which are found in every facet of the business, from vision and strategy to on-time delivery and returns. The types of properties that are the "musts" on the list are speed, flexibility, customer focus, and intellectual capital. But these properties are not always easy to measure in and of themselves, so we need to deal with the attributes of these properties. They manifest themselves in such things as cycle times, on-time delivery, and customer retention rates. The big step is to develop measurements for all of these attributes.

Take customer retention as an example. "On average the CEOs of U.S. corporations lose half their customers every five years. This fact shocks most people. It shocks the CEOs themselves, most of whom have little insight into the causes of the customer exodus, let alone the cures, because they do not measure customer defections.... Good, long-standing customers are worth so much that in some industries, reducing customer defections by as little as five points—from, say, 15 percent to 10 percent per year—can *double* profits."[7] This thinking led "Deere & Company, which makes John Deere tractors, to nearly 98 percent annual customer retention in some product areas."[8]

Measurement Hierarchy

The right measurement system can in itself become a change agent, working in real time throughout the organization. It begins with an overall performance view of the organization that provides a means of seeing all the key measures that drive performance. It's a hierarchical view that requires special thoughtware *and* software.

First the thoughtware. Put together a cross-functional team whose mandate is to build a new measurement and navigational system, and imbue it in the new thoughtware. Again, one of the most effective ways of gaining insight and knowledge is to simulate the realities of your business. Take five days and jump in with the whole team.

In Just Five Working Days:
- Revisit and confirm with senior management the organization's vision and case for action.
- Set the team's mandate.
- Take the team members through all they need to know about the new measurement concepts, technical information (how the software works), and application (how to build the measurement hierarchy).
- Gather the needed information.
- Validate the information.
- Install a database.

First step accomplished. The team has engaged new thoughtware, the hierarchy is designed, and the information is in a database. The result is the rudimentary beginnings of a whole new measurement and navigational system. Next, develop a pilot program that brings the database (the information) to life, then make it available to the rest of the organization. Establish regular (daily, weekly, monthly) dialogue on the information in the database, its contribution to navigational issues, its use, and its relevance to those who have to use it (from CEO and CFO to supervisors and shippers). Use the pilot program to create a dynamic annealing process for the information. The pilot will open up—and heat up—communications. The annealing of the information will become an ongoing process, reaching into every nook and cranny of the organization, continually validating, changing, and adapting the information. Feedback like, "That measurement is of no use," and,

"That doesn't tell me what's best to do next," and "I have no idea what I'm measured on," will be invaluable in building the system. And it will happen constantly. Now you're navigating, not just measuring.

With the new thoughtware firmly embedded, the departmentalized thinking disappears. Information becomes the basis of clear communication—free moving, common to all—and everyone focuses on unified direction. This is *not* a central computer information system; we know they don't navigate. This is a decentralized, dispersed, adaptive information system combining new thoughtware and new software. This is a master navigational system that everyone is tied in to.

Measuring Total Capital

New measurement thoughtware is inextricably linked to the concept of *total capital,* and it is imperative that the organization's measurement and navigational system relates to every facet of its total capital. Charles Savage, in his book *Fifth Generation Management,* articulates the concept and importance of total capital as well as anyone. In addition to financial capital, the capital in a business (defined as any source of profit, advantage, asset, or leverage to create value) is made up of assets, both tangible and intangible. *The combination of financial capital, tangible assets, and intellectual (intangible) assets is known as total capital.* The financial and tangible we know well; however, *the intellectual capital is where we have failed in our attempt to measure and manage properly*—if at all—and yet this is where so much of the value lies in the organization. The *intellectual capital* is the sum of *human, structural, and customer capital* (see Figure 7-4).

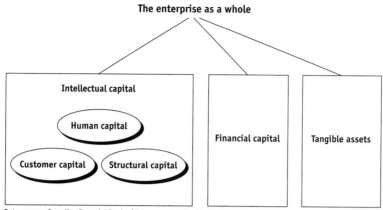

Data source: Canadian Imperial Bank of Commerce Leadership Center

Figure 7-4. What Is Intellectual Capital?

Most organizations are only getting at the tip of the iceberg by measuring their financial capital. As illustrated in Figure 7-5, the three components of intellectual capital are the hidden—but no less important—90 percent.

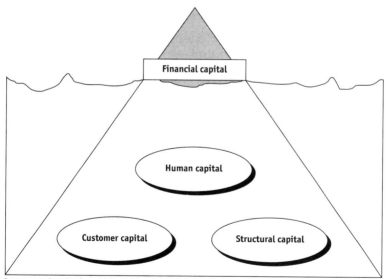

Data source: Canadian Imperial Bank of Commerce Leadership Center

Figure 7-5. Iceberg Balance Sheet

Intellectual capital is different from tangible capital (see Table 7-1), and inherent in it are many barriers and stumbling blocks to measuring intangibles. For example, much of it is invisible, difficult to quantify, and seldom tracked through traditional accounting. It has a short life when not in use and is usually assessed (measured) based on assumptions—and therefore not reliable. On the other hand, intellectual capital has many positives and can be a significant value contributor: It can't be bought, sold, or imitated; it appreciates with purposeful use, offers multi-application value, and can be greatly leveraged through directional alignment.

Table 7-1. Tangible Assets Versus Intellectual Capital

Tangible Assets (Required for business operations)	Intellectual Capital (Key to competitive advantage in the knowledge era)
• Readily visible • Rigorously quantified • Part of the balance sheet • Investment produces known returns • Can be easily duplicated • Depreciates with use • Has finite application • Best managed with "scarcity" mentality • Best leveraged through control • Can be accumulated and stored	• Invisible • Difficult to quantify • Not tracked through accounting • Assessment based on assumptions • Cannot be bought, or imitated • Appreciates with purposeful use • Multi-application without reducing value • Best managed with "abundance" mentality • Best leveraged through alignment • Dynamic: short self-life when not in use

Data source: Canadian Imperial Bank of Commerce Leadership Center

The Dynamics of Intellectual Capital

Intellectual capital is the roadbed of the highway to the future. Without it as the underlying foundation, the road ahead is downhill to nowhere. Intellectual capital is where the real, sustainable competitive advantage can be built, must be built.

The value of an organization's intellectual capital is driven by the interaction of the three components—human, structural, customer (see Figure 7-6). This value is determined by the effectiveness, and the dynamic nature, of the organization's processes because it is process that connects, synergizes, and magnifies the relationship among the three. The better and the faster the organization's processes, the greater the value, thus the competitive advantage.

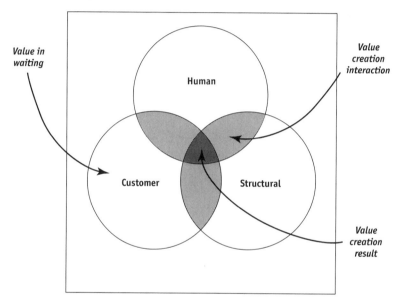

Figure 7-6. The Dynamics of Intellectual Capital

Human Capital

Human capital refers to the capability of individuals to produce solutions for customers. It includes such attributes as commitment to the organization, level of initiative, individual learning capability, ability to relate, ability to create, and investment in human resource development. The value of human capital is at a high conversion rate when the organization is flexible, redeploys resources quickly, initiates versus reacts, and is good at managing conflict and dysfunctionality.

Structural Capital

Structural capital refers to the capabilities of the organization to meet market demands. It includes systems, products, cultures, structures, logistics, and strategies, as well as the ability to capture opportunities. For example, when a company can deliver product in 30 days instead of 120 days, the value of its structural capital is infinitely better than before. With the application of new thoughtware, some companies have gotten rid of everyone at the head office except the president. One such group spun off the old head office into a group that has now taken responsibility for managing and supplying structural capital to the rest of the organization. Inherent in this process is the maximization of the value of the structural capital. In increasing the value of structural capital, many companies convert their synchronized flow into smaller modules that can be easily accessed, redeployed, and reconfigured.

Customer Capital

Customer capital refers to the depth/penetration, width/coverage, attachment/loyalty, and profitability of customers. It is enhanced by the degree the organization is co-creating solutions with customers versus just selling them product. Some organizations co-design products, while others are in partnership with customers. When customers simply call in and order on price, the customer capital is only slightly above nothing.

When customers are "partnering" in creating multiple business solutions, then the customer capital is high.

Managing and Measuring Total Capital

With a full-view measurement hierarchy in place, and the right navigational system, the organization can measure and manage its total capital. The goal is to increase the total capital value of the organization by aligning the components of intellectual capital, along with its financial capital and tangible assets. The increased value generated by such a system can provide a major competitive advantage.

In bringing the components together, there are a number of organizational factors, or characteristics, to be dealt with. Tables 7-2, 7-3, and 7-4 list the main factors that are either conducive to enhancing value or detracting from it for each of the three combinations of intellectual capital.

Table 7-2. Structural/Human Factors

Value attractors	Value detractors
• Shared sense of purpose • Entrepreneurial culture fostering individual initiative • Cohesiveness through "strategic bonding" • Alignment of strategic capability elements • Dynamic leadership/managerial courage • Speed of change/agility • Emphasis on learning	• Segmented (stovepipe) organization • Bureaucratic barriers • Prescriptive/overcontrolling center • High proportion of low customer value activity • Lack of customer visibility • Lack of internal coherence • Strategic confusion

Data source: Canadian Imperial Bank of Commerce Leadership Center

Table 7-3. Structural/Customer Factors

Value attractors	Value detractors
• Well-tuned business processes • Win-win service orientation to customer • Simplified/streamlined structure aligned to customer relationships • "Harvesting" as opposed to distribution perspective • Customer learning an inherent part of services • Products are the building blocks for innovative solutions for the customer	• Inefficient or ineffective processes not geared to the customer • Lack of connection/feedback loops with customers • Internally-generated turbulence • Insufficient or inaccurate technical support • Predominance of "product" orientation versus "solution" orientation

Data source: Canadian Imperial Bank of Commerce Leadership Center

Table 7-4. Human/Customer Factors

Value attractors	Value detractors
• Personal responsibility perspective • Customer focus/service orientation • Active learning • Continuity in role • Commitment to shared purpose • Ownership for one's part in the enterprise • Co-creative solutions	• Internal preoccupation • Competency gaps • Inability to relate to customers • Lack of strategic clarity

Data source: Canadian Imperial Bank of Commerce Leadership Center

Motivation and Measurement: Inseparable Partners

There is no bigger motivator than a clear, relevant, and consistent objective.

Without relevant measurement there is no means of motivation. The new thoughtware on measurement goes a long way toward dissolving the two often mentioned problems of motivation that are reflected in the refrains, "Communication stinks around here," and "What's in it for me?" Now the organization, through its new navigational and fully networked system, can answer these important questions. The network carries all the necessary information and it is easily accessed; therefore, no one can validly say that "communication stinks." It is up to individuals to access and configure the information into the communication needed so that they understand *what, when,* and *where.* The onus is on the individual to plug in and use the navigational system, and to perform accordingly. If the information is off, or if the individual's readings of the information are unclear, or it's inconsistent with organizational direction, then this becomes clearly communicated, and it allows someone to pursue a different course and find a solution. The result is that the communication problem is largely resolved because it has been converted to an informational disbursement issue, and the responsibility (and the ability) to resolve the issue has been placed with each and every individual. It allows for the setting of clear and relevant objectives that are consistently aligned with both the individual's and organization's purpose.

Now everyone is focused and the setting of priorities and the allocation of resources is done within the same context. Everyone is rowing in the same direction, or they know the reason why they're not. This gives the organization the wherewithal to answer the second question, "What's in it for me?" With proper measures, a compensation system can be fashioned that meets the very tangible and clear objectives of both the individual and the organization. The drivers of the business are known and understood; therefore, the reward can be a direct link between performance drivers and individuals, and between the core elements of intangible capital and the organization's goals. This is where the pyramid of relevant measures (Figure 7-2) applies by linking detailed individual measures and objectives with the larger company measures and objectives.

With a measurement system that is truly navigational, and directly related to key motivation factors, the organization can now focus on the most important factor: the customer.

Notes

[1] Thomas Stewart, "Intellectual Capital," *Fortune,* October 3, 1994, p. 68.

[2] James Quinn, Philip Anderson, Sydney Finkelstein, "Managing Professional Intellect: Making the Most of the Best," *Harvard Business Review,* March–April 1996, p. 75.

[3] Ibid., p. 77.

[4] Ibid., p. 77.

[5] Jeremy Rifkin, *The End of Work* (New York: G.P. Putnam's Sons, 1995), p. 61.

[6] Saul Wurman, *Information Anxiety* (as quoted in *New Work Habits for a Radically Changing World,* p. 21).

[7] Frederick Reichheld, "Learning from Customer Defections," *Harvard Business Review,* March–April 1996, p. 56.

[8] Ibid., p. 69.

A Focus on Time to Action | **8**

Jack be nimble, Jack be quick . . .
or someone else will be.

Span of Control Is Obsolete

Span of control has been a prime architect in the construction of bureaucracy, and over the years each has served the other well. As we said in Chapter IV, we are not talking here about hierarchy, for it should not be mistaken for span of control. Hierarchy is necessary in the organization in order to create and link managerial relationships and their respective authority and accountability, but hierarchy does not have to, nor should it, create bureaucracy.

Years ago automobile manufacturers strove to back-integrate their business into steel—indeed, all the way back to the iron ore mines—so they could control the raw material supply. It was all in pursuit of advantage, based on economies of scale, but today velocity is where the advantage is to be gained. Today, back-integration can be cumbersome and time consuming, and span of control is counterproductive. Historically, as the economies of scale boomed and organizations grew, span of control was central to the flow of information and the meting out of authority. Even with industrial decentralization, span of control was necessary to manage the ebb and flow of business up and down the layers of management.

But today, span of control is no longer a requisite. Technology, and the proliferation of information, has made it not only obsolete but destructive as well. Span of control blocks information alignment and inhibits the full use of knowledge. Information doesn't need bureaucracy to move it; we can tap in literally anywhere, anytime (especially when we've designed a new navigational measurement system) to get what we need to know. In fact, because information is instantaneous and knowledge pervasive, we need to redesign the organization around velocity. Speed dictates, and from it arises new networks, new concepts, and new thoughtware.

Redesigning with New Thoughtware

Most organizations are designed around the three imperatives of *time, cost,* and *value/quality.* To date, we've beaten on costs and improved quality to the point that they are givens in the game, and while doing so we have always held time as a constant. This is where new thoughtware comes into play. Time is not a constant; in fact, it is the largest variable cost in the organization and offers tremendous leverage potential in the process of change. We know time consists of an enormous amount of non-value-added activity—real costs—that can be eliminated, thus dramatically decreasing costs and increasing speed. It's a double hit. And with speed as the mandate, quality is inherent because it has to be right the first time.

We've known about this "time thing" for some time, but we haven't found a sustained way of getting at it. (Even cycle time reduction is only part of the solution: A study cited in a *Harvard Business Review* article found that even though "complete-process departments" reduced cycle times significantly the organization's performance did not improve, and in some cases declined.[1]) Redesigning on the issue of velocity is a speed tactic. It doesn't mean running faster, however; it means removing the hurdles to greater velocity, thereby reducing the non-valued activity. This allows the organization to build the capability of *instantaneous response to customized demand*—this is the new thoughtware, and it requires a laser-like focus on the customer (see Figure 8-1).

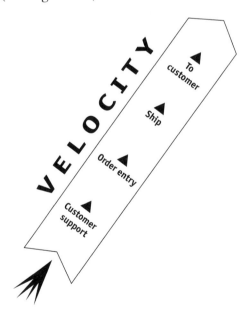

Figure 8-1. Velocity

Focus on Customer Value

Everything the organization does is geared toward enhancing the value we deliver to the customer, and in delivering instantaneous response to customized demand we have to change almost every aspect of the operations. One change that is paramount is moving the point of variance, or the point of decision, as far downstream as possible. The closer to the customer it is, the faster the response.

A great example of moving the point of variance farther downstream with a focus on time to action is that of Andersen Windows, a $1 billion, Minnesota-based company. In the early 1980s Andersen was a mass producer of a wide range of windows. As consumers asked for more and more unique windows, Andersen tried to keep up with the custom options. The catalogues expanded and so did the time it took retailers to spec and quote the product for customers. This growing complexity led to a concomitantly growing error rate: As the number of products increased from 28,000 in 1985 to 86,000 in 1991, 20 percent of all truckloads contained at least one order discrepancy—double the 1985 error rate.

In the early 1990s Andersen changed its strategy from mass production to customer-focused mass customization. It sold its retailers on installing an interactive computer version of the catalogue, which allowed sales people and customers to change features until they had essentially custom designed the window they wanted. The computer then generated a price quote. At a price of approximately $4,000 per installation, by 1996 Andersen had 650 in place. Then Andersen linked the retail computer with the factory and tracked each order from assembly line to warehouse. In 1995 Andersen shipped 188,000 different products with errors in fewer than one in 200 truck-loads. Andersen has changed the ground rules of competition, all emanating from a focus on customer needs and velocity. And they're not finished. The next step in mass customization for Andersen is what they call batch-of-one manufacturing, aimed at drastically lowering the inventory of finished window parts. A pilot project was underway by 1996.[2]

Mass customization is becoming the way business is done in more and more companies. For example, National Bicycle Industrial Company in Kokubu, Japan, builds custom bicycles on an assembly line, but you can order any one of 11 million variations of its models to suit your taste, at prices only 10 percent higher than the mass-produced, non-customized models.[3] Similarly, insurer U.S.AA does almost all customer service by telephone. The company scans 40,000 pages of mail each day into a paperless system from which service reps can access any document during a phone call with any customer. As a result, customers get immediate answers to their questions and nothing ever gets lost.[4] Unfortunately, these companies are still the exception rather than the rule, even though the rule changed years ago. The vast majority of organizations are still struggling to get their collective heads around the concept of instantaneous, mass customization. They're still running on old thoughtware (and software).

Getting Fast

So what does the rethought, redesigned, fast, flexible, and focused organization look like? It can be described in different ways, but we like the terminology Kevin Kelly uses in his book *Out of Control*. He argues that such an organization must inherently be *distributed, decentralized, collaborative,* and *adaptive.*[5] We've added our thinking to these terms in Figure 8-2.

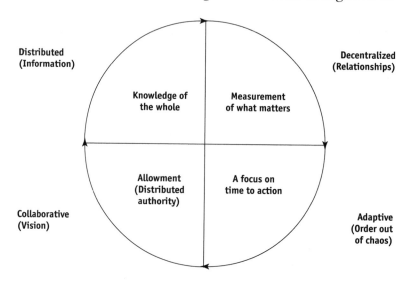

Figure 8-2. Four Components of the New Organization

Distributed

The distributed organization is one based on *teaming,* which is different thoughtware than forming and joining teams. In the new thoughtware, teaming is a *process* in which people don't only join a team, *they experience teaming.* It's like the misunderstanding of leadership, where the thought is I am a leader, rather than I am getting others to see the vision, embrace the goal, and move toward it. The latter is the *process* of leadership. Likewise, teaming is a way of thinking, a process. It is a way of continually understanding context and creating the best possible content for that particular context—always changing content to fit changing context.

John Katzenbach and Douglas Smith, in their book *The Wisdom of Teams,* emphasize that the single most important factor that differentiates successful from unsuccessful teams is having "meaningful purpose." To imbed this in a distributed organization there must be a common approach, specific goals, and the appropriate skills.

The distributed organization requires a mind-set of teaming that is widely distributed—one that can be mentally, physically, or technologically in many places concurrently, work in small groups, configure and reconfigure rapidly, and always be clear on performance measurement and individual accountability. Teaming allows the organization to become distributed (therefore more responsive and faster), but it does not usurp or bypass the essential question of accountability. There is always someone accountable. There *cannot* be collective or team accountability, only individual accountability, and it must always rest with the team leader or project manager or whoever is ultimately accountable for the team. When the task is complete, the accountability is measured, and then the team disbands. But the thoughtware of teaming is continuous, and it's all about thinking that understands and responds to context. If you want to have a distributed organization, learn it, apply it, live by it.

Decentralized

The new decentralized thinking is a far cry from decentralization in the Alfred Sloan era. Most of the latter structuring (still in wide use today) is anchored in old, decentralized span of control thoughtware in which the truism "bigger is better" is just one of many drastically wrong assumptions. In today's context, on the other hand, the *paradox of control* says that the less control we have, the more control we have over our success. This is because decentralized thoughtware is based on separating the "what" from the "how." If the organization has properly answered what business it is in, what its core competencies are, and what it wants to be in the future, then the how will follow just as naturally as a river follows a path to the sea. And decentralized thinking focuses on the river, thus giving the organization the power, the flexibility, and the speed to respond. Clarify the what, separate the how, and install this kind of decentralized thoughtware, everywhere.

Collaborative

As a concept, collaboration is not new; we have been forming strategic alliances and partnerships for years. However, in the new context it has much greater implications. It used to be that senior management negotiated strategic alliances and decided in which partnerships to participate. But now, in the world of speed, everyone has to be thinking about, and creating, collaborative relationships. In. Out. Change. Renegotiate. Reconfigure. It's the way business is done, and unless the organization installs a motherboard of collaborative thoughtware the only speed to be experienced will be how fast the competition pulls away.

Ace Hardware owner Bob Curry quickly adopted collaborative thinking when a huge Home Depot opened up a quarter of a mile away from his store. Curry made several smart moves, but none better than collaborating with "the enemy": now Home Depot refers customers to his store for service problems. "We work to build some kind of bond between Home Depot and us rather than try to fight," says Curry.[6] Great thinking.

Collaboration has fostered outsourcing, supplier partnering, the unlikely alliance between IBM and Apple, and the likes of airline, retail, and bank credit cards and point programs. In the external market, we're just beginning to see the tip of the iceberg. Internally, collaborative thinking is stymied by old thoughtware—as evidenced by the thousands of teams and process-complete departments that have not been able to produce the expected results—because everything changed except the thoughtware and therefore real collaboration never took place. Push the collaborative thinking way past the normal boundaries of business thinking if you want to break mind-sets and change behavior. Instill it, encourage it, let everyone do it.

Adaptive

Being adaptive is something the dinosaurs in the Mesozoic era didn't think much about, and there are plenty of dinosauric organizations in the current millennium that haven't thought much about it either. Adaptive is a *must* characteristic of any organization that expects to exist in the future. The accelerating onslaught of knowledge and information, and the sheer velocity of change, make being adaptive almost more of an instinct than a developed trait. Jan Leschly, chief executive of SmithKline Beecham, underscored the importance of adaptiveness about a year after being put in charge of the worldwide pharmaceutical business:

> There were about 12 people on my management team. Today, I have to admit there are only 2 of them left. It was a gradual process. Some people retired; some didn't think the job was fun any longer; a few enjoyed it and stayed. We found we needed people who were capable of adapting to a

completely new way of running the business and who weren't wedded to either of the premerger cultures.[7]

The thoughtware of adaptiveness must handle, at any point, at any time, the turbulence in demand, the ever-shifting costs, the intensity of information, and the sensitivity of human capital (culture). At the core of adaptivity is learning, and it draws from all the information, knowledge, and skills available. Provide the opportunity for people to maximize their natural capability of adaptiveness (many have it, and will show it *if* the thoughtware changes), so they can properly and positively deal with the ever-changing circumstances and environment around them.

Rapid Deployment

An innate understanding of the four cornerstones we have discussed above is the beginning of velocity redesign, but you still have to make them happen. There are several different methods of deployment—Workouts, Rapid JIT, Gemba Blitz, JIT Blitz, and so on. The method we like best is taken from a framework designed by the Deltapoint Corporation, a very progressive west coast-based firm. We've outlined our version of it on the next two pages. Take any portion of the business (or all of it) and simulate four quarters of business— your facts, your information, your people—then apply the thoughtware of the four components of redesign. See what can happen. Experience the speed of change. Next, do it for real. Take a discrete cell of the business and put together a four-phase, rapid deployment project based on the new velocity thoughtware:

Phase I. Rapid Deployment Assessment

Opportunity
- Product flow
- Processes
- Equipment
- Demand level

Readiness
- Need for improvement
- Enthusiasm
- Culture

Phase II. Rapid Deployment Planning

Boundaries of the process

Management education and expectations
- Purpose and process
- Desired outcomes

Team selection
- Representative of the process
- Key stakeholders

Detailed plan and data collection

Phase III. Rapid Deployment Implementation

Simulate and learn the principles, analyze and identify key
    opportunities

Review current methods, set out vision of successful imple-
    mentation and action plan

Apply new methods and begin implementation

Implementation complete: Compare results and develop
    next steps

Phase IV. Rapid Deployment Deployment

Hold the gains
- Standardization
- Replication of best practices

Move forward
- Complete the open action items
- Expand to more areas

- Connect islands of improvement
- Address systems level issues

Impacts of Rapid Deployment

Create commitment for improvement—show it can be done rapidly

Make breakthrough improvements as a part of larger system change

Develop a bias for taking action on what is learned

Operationalize allowment—no longer words, but action

Rapid Deployment's Key Characteristics

Transfer of knowledge
- Not consultant-dependent

People rapidly learn and apply principles
- Learn why and how, not just what

People make their own improvements
- It's not done to them or for them; they do it for themselves, creating ownership

Build improved systems
- Not islands of change

Flexible model from broad to focused events

Results: The Real Case of a Large Manufacturer

A Complex Wire Design Process
- Eliminated non-value-added steps
- Created white collar work cells
- Reduce travel distance from 82,900 ft. to 7,200 ft (–91%)
- Reduced hand-offs from 733 to 91 (–88%)
- Reduced flowtime average days from 63 to 40 (–37%)
- Reduced non-value-added hours from 15,400 to 7,400 (–52%)

The difference between other rapid improvement programs and the type we are suggesting here is in what the injection of new thoughtware does: It creates *contextual change,* thereby overcoming the problem of simply implementing new content in the same context.

The idea of rapid improvement allows people to compact the principles of redesign into a focused, self-contained project, and then apply new thoughtware. Companies are getting started in as short a time as *one week*. Some take six to eight weeks, but the results are the same: extraordinary. In some offices (e.g., the information department) they knock down the walls, sit in groups, move equipment, and in a week are processing information in 20 minutes that previously took two days. And doing in a day what use to take a week. It's that dramatic and that quick.

This type of improvement demonstrates first-hand what the new thoughtware can do. Doing begets doing. From one rapid improvement project the organization can leapfrog ahead, replicating the new practices and expanding to system-level changes.

Getting to the End

The road to comprehensive installation of new thoughtware goes through span of control, and the organization can only achieve velocity when the span of control is obliterated. From here, the transformation begins to take hold with the application of the new thoughtware of knowledge, measurement, and velocity. *Then* the organization is entitled to move to allowment.

Notes

[1] Ann Majchrzak and Qianwei Wang, "Breaking the Functional Mind-Set in Process Organizations," *Harvard Business Review*, September–October 1996, p. 93.

[2] Justin Martin, "Are You As Good As You Think You Are?" *Fortune,* September 30, 1996, p. 142.

[3] Kevin Kelly, *Out of Control* (Reading, MA: Addison-Wesley, 1994), pp. 189–193.

[4] Dick Schaaf, *Keeping the Edge* (New York: Dutton/Penguin Books, 1995).

[5] Kevin Kelly, *Out of Control* (Reading, MA: Addison-Wesley, 1994). pp. 189–193.

[6] Guy Kawasaki, *How to Drive Your Competition Crazy* (New York: Hyperion, 1995).

[7] David Garvin, "Leveraging Processes for Strategic Advantage," *Harvard Business Review,* September–October 1995, p. 83.

Allowment

9

When you're entitled, you're allowed.

The differential between empowered and non-empowered groups is flatlining, doing nothing, zero, zilch. It's obvious, isn't it, that we aren't *all* empowered, despite the fact that we've been trying empowerment for a couple of decades or more? Why? Because it's been nothing more than a congo line of programs marching down the aisles of ivory towers and bustling plants trying to do what can't be done: trying to empower people before they're entitled to be empowered; giving people all the training and encouragement required, but never the authority—because we've never been comfortable with releasing authority. So empowerment has been a half-baked cake, and it's left more than a bad taste in our mouth. That's why we make the distinction between empowerment and allowment.

Forget the thought of someone empowering someone else. Instead, think a new thought. Think of *allowing everyone to do whatever they want*. It sounds risky, and it goes against all we know about control, but it's not risky if we look at it in the new context of information access and knowledge. The new context conjures new thoughts. It moves the thinking to If we let people do what they want, what do we have to change in order *not* to create total chaos? It focuses on the individual being capable of doing whatever is necessary. It focuses on having the point of decision as far downstream as possible. It focuses on distributed accountability. It goes beyond programmatic empowerment (which moves power from one person to another without ever dealing with the process of entitlement) and focuses on an individual who has the information, skills, *and* authority to do whatever is necessary.

> *The worst thing you can do is empower an organization that is not entitled to be empowered.*

There's much being done in this critical area, and more and more organizations see allowment as an important component in the new context. They're making it a key strategy for growth (it's funny how the same names come to mind: FedEx, Honda, Microsoft, all leaders). It begins with a true understanding of the value and role of human capital in the new context, the value of individuals to provide innovation and solutions for customers—something "Chainsaw" Al Dunlap didn't understand when he tore through Scott Paper and Sunbeam.

The new context has a different perspective on where and how value is generated. It poses a fundamental question about how important people are in creating true, long-term value.

What's technology and information without human capital? Do you take people and treat them as an investment? Are they an asset on the balance sheet or an expense item on the P&L? If they're an expense, then don't think you can empower them. If you consider your people as an investment, if your training budgets are capitalized, if your employees are depreciated as other assets are, if your human capital is managed like an asset and allowed to maximize its return to shareholders (which is what senior management is accountable for), then you understand allowment.

If this asset is not providing an adequate return, then the first question should not be what's wrong with the asset, but rather why is senior management not getting the most out of this asset? Because they are accountable for human capital's performance? This is a critical principle of allowment: Management is accountable for the hiring, training, development, and outputs of the people who work for them, and if the effectiveness of the resource (the people) is judged to be insufficient, then *it is management that is accountable, not the resource.* It's management's role to generate, develop, sustain, and reward the organization's core competencies. If there's a problem, don't throw out the resource, look to management and determine if the resource has been allowed to maximize its potential, its effectiveness. The answer, nine times out of ten, is no.

Far too often management does not allow the resource, the human capital, to perform to its potential. What does management do instead? It blames the resource, fiddles with it (more training, more teaming), tries to empower it more (without more authority), squeezes it, and eventually downsizes it. And then it carries right on doing the same old thing, in the same old structure, with the same old thinking. It should be self-evident in a world that is demanding more and more knowledge and innovation—all totally dependent on the value of the available human capital—that we should be keeping, accumulating, and investing in human capital, and then allowing it to grow, build, and multiply. It is the foundation of the future.

Admit it or not, business is about *more* than piling up profits. At Servicemaster, profits are a means to an end, and nowhere is this better stated than by company chairman C. William Pollard in his book, *The Soul of the Firm:*

> In the past twenty years the company has grown twenty times larger and employs 200,000 people serving 6 million customers in thirty countries. For every six cents it invests, it generates a dollar of revenue, and return on equity has averaged 50 percent. ... If profit is the end and not the means, if profits are piled up instead of used, then the people of the firm eventually lose their direction and purpose—resulting in the eventual loss of customers and thus the loss of profits.[1]

Robert Herres, chairman and CEO of United Services Automobile Association (USAA) also clearly understands the value of human capital: "We want to keep our employees when we shift to new processes. They come with assets like loyalty, commitment to customers, and understanding of our culture and our mission.[2]

Allowment is about aligning organizational and human goals whereby the people do what's best for the purpose and goals of the organization because it's the same as doing what's best for themselves. First Tennessee National Corp. started taking family issues seriously, treating them as strategic business questions. The bank got rid of a lot of work rules and let the employees figure out which schedules worked best—

"because they know what needs to be done, both on and off the job," says Becky Tipton, a department supervisor. After training, clear gains in productivity and customer service emerged. As employees got control over their workplace, "managers had to change the way they did business," says CEO Ralph Horn.[3]

> *The people who do the work know what to do*
> *to satisfy the customer, so allow them to do it.*

Getting Things in Place

Empowerment as a program ignored the fundamental requirement that people must be entitled before they can be empowered. As an aside, we would normally have no problem with the interchangeability of the two words *empowerment* and *allowment,* except empowerment is so encrusted with erroneous perceptions and old thoughtware that it carries forward too many false implications. In addition, the lessons learned from the widespread failure of empowerment have given us new principles to embed in allowment. So, we leave empowerment behind, and think in terms of allowment.

Entitlement

Entitlement is a non-negotiable condition of allowment. Entitlement isn't benchmark (eventually benchmark is the goal), it's less—for two very good reasons. First, it is unrealistic to set out to achieve benchmark right from the get-go; that instills far more pessimism than optimism. Second, reaching benchmark always requires a significant investment of additional resources, thereby encumbering the entire process with major, resource/capital decisions in the early going. Conversely, with entitlement as a first step, the organization can move ahead quickly, positively, and decisively while creating a goal that is usually 50–70 percent of benchmark. Not bad for starters.

• How Good Do You Need to Be? •

Changing a flat tire is not one of life's looking-forward-to tasks, but neither is it a monumental undertaking for most of us. When it's necessary, however, it's something you want to get done, be efficient about, and be on your way as soon as possible—not to mention avoid the grime and dirt. You want to be fast and clean, but how fast? The benchmark for changing a tire is about 13 seconds, accomplished by professional race car pit crews. It would be great to have your tire changed in 13 seconds, or even 60 or 120 seconds, and never touch it, but at what cost, at what effort?

It's quite impractical to think of carrying the required equipment and crew around to enable you to change a tire in such a time frame. However, you certainly could reduce the change time from around 10–12 minutes to under 5 minutes, and reduce the chances of getting dirty, with a little practice, a few new techniques, and a pair of gloves and coveralls. The five minutes is entitlement—what you can reach without any additional capital investment; the 13 seconds is benchmark—requiring a significant capital investment.

Three Prerequisites of Allowment

The organization cannot reach entitlement or benchmark until it understands how to create allowment. First, it must have clearly stated the organization's meaningful purpose, relevant objectives, and a case for action. Then it must meet the three prerequisites of information, skills, and authority.

Information

First and foremost, there must be information—the right information, in the right place, at the right time. Most organizations are woefully short on this one issue alone. They aren't even at first base on this requirement, so it's no wonder most have failed at empowerment. They have not installed the capability, the connections, the communications, or the systems to properly inform. Even if the information systems are in place, too many are not integrated, and most are one way, not two way, which means it's not real communication. Today organizations have the technology (or they had better get it), but they still have not supplied the right thoughtware to transform information and become entitled to create allowment.

Information is more than just a good idea; it should be an inherent strategy with the potential to be a powerful, competitive weapon. From the Internet to intranets, we have the capability to tie any and all relevant information together, to connect, distribute, collaborate, collate, retrieve, update, and communicate constantly. With technology (structure capital) our human capital has the opportunity to be truly empowered, *if allowed*. Again, one of the reasons empowerment failed was because those newly empowered did not have, or have access to, the required information.

Skills

Once the information *is* in place, then it becomes a matter of using it. Knowing how to access it. Knowing how to analyze it.

Knowing what to do with it. Understanding it. Understanding the company strategies and objectives. Understanding the performance drivers. It takes skills, and skills require learning (more on this in a moment). Whether the organization likes it or not, information is abundant, so the people must have the required skills to use it properly—how to turn information into knowledge, how to use it, where to apply it. Skill development is a one-way street to growth, with two lanes. In one lane is the individual wanting and willing to build skills and invest the required commitment. In the other lane is the organization wanting to increase the value in its human capital and willing to invest in it. Together skill development becomes a major goal, one without the other and it's a grid lock.

Authority

The authority to act is at the heart of allowment, and it is the single most bastardized prerequisite. There's no lack of authority, but prying it out of where it is, and moving it to where it should be, is like trying to move icebergs with an ice pick. Authority is the last bastion of power in empowerment. When empowering, many a manager provides a lot of information and skill training, but never gives up authority. They don't have the guts to give it up—they can't because they're stuck in old thoughtware. So, the empowerment programs generate a week's worth of substance and a year's worth of frustration. In reallocating authority, an obvious caveat is that authority should not be moved until the information and skills are in place. Also, keep in mind that no one has authority until two things happen: (1) the authority is assigned to an individual, and (2) that person has the *capability* to carry out the authority. If not, the authority is quickly undermined.

The downfall of empowerment was too much of the first and not enough of the latter.

If the people have the requisite information and skills, then the movement of authority from where it is to where it should be is natural and easy.

Individual Entitlement

The organization cannot reach its entitlement until a sufficient number of people have reached individual entitlement. Entitlement begins with the thinking that people in the organization can, and should, be capable of doing whatever they want—once they have the needed information, skills, and authority. This pulls the organization into creating a process that allows people to build their entitlement in line with what the organization wants and needs. At the core of the process of individual entitlement are two concepts: skill development and partnering.

Skill Development

In the past, skill development has too often been no more than training made available as part of an overall, all-encompassing, all-nebulous "learning program." Certainly, the What's in it for me? question was seldom answered, and a methodology for self-fulfillment and continual assessment was conspicuously absent. Where it all led to, nobody knew. The new thought-ware is based on the premise that people want to, can, and will, expand their capability—their skills—if given the right opportunity in the right context (opportunity in the wrong context is really no opportunity at all). Allowment creates the context, and the organization has the responsibility to provide the opportunity.

The term "partnering" is being more widely used and is a manifestation of allowment. Ask the question, Is the organization partnering? Ask if it is allowing for the accomplishment of necessary tasks while promoting an individual sense of ownership, an understanding of the broader aspects of the business, and a gaining of experience in non-traditional areas of responsibilities? The answer should be, Yes, yes, yes. In the list that follows is an example of some of the ingredients of partnering being employed by a large midwest manufacturer.

- A partnership must be necessary work. It should never be "make work."
- A partnership should be work that goes beyond the traditional expectations of the job title/description of the employee.
- A partnership must have a definite purpose, objectives, and measurable criteria.
- A partnership is a team responsibility. The successful performance of the partnership is an important part of the employee's responsibilities.
- A partnership should take an average of less than one hour a week. Total partnerships for any individual should not require more than four hours per week.
- A partnership should normally not be time critical (there will be exceptions).
- Partnership participation and performance should be considered in performance reviews.
- Partnerships will be assigned and defined by the partnership coordinator.

Everyone has the responsibility to achieve individual entitlement because if a person is not entitled to perform required tasks (i.e., does not have the needed information, skills, and authority), then their value is less than required. The goal is for the individual to be of value and to be continually requested to participate in the ever-changing organization. If you're not a valued resource, you're not likely to be requested. Then, as the saying goes, "You're toast." Much goes into building a person's entitlement, and allowment places the onus on the people to become entitled, but it's the organization's responsibility to make available, to all, the opportunity and resources needed to build entitlement.

Getting to Individual Entitlement

The organization needs to provide a framework, a process, and tools with which the individual can build his or her career. This framework must include the necessary guidelines, coaching, and mentoring; relevant requirements for all areas; and a managerial means of assessment. The organization should set out clear guidelines for all. Coaching should be done regularly by those with expertise and capability in each particular area. Mentors should be managers at least one level above an individual's current boss, who are familiar with the area an individual is working in and have the scope to relate cross-organization, growth opportunities. The individual must be aware of the requirements and value of the position/area he or she is currently in or is interested in.

Finally, there must be a balanced and clear means of assessment. An example of such an assessment tool is shown in the following illustrations (from the same midwest manufacturer). Figure 9-1 depicts a simplified example of three categories representing judgments of an individual's current capability: E = Exposed but must have guidance, A = can work Alone, and C = training is Complete. These ratings are based on an assessment committee's review of the individual's skill levels in designated categories. The production activity-management skill set requirements for a production scheduler are shown in Table 9-1. The ratings are then applied in Table 9-2. For example, J. Jones received an E rating in "customer needs analysis," meaning Jones has been exposed to this skill but must have continuous guidance in order to carry it out. The ratings (judgments) are used by the assessment committee, which includes the individual's current manager and manager one level up, who discuss with the person his or her career development.

Skill sets, sub sets, description elements

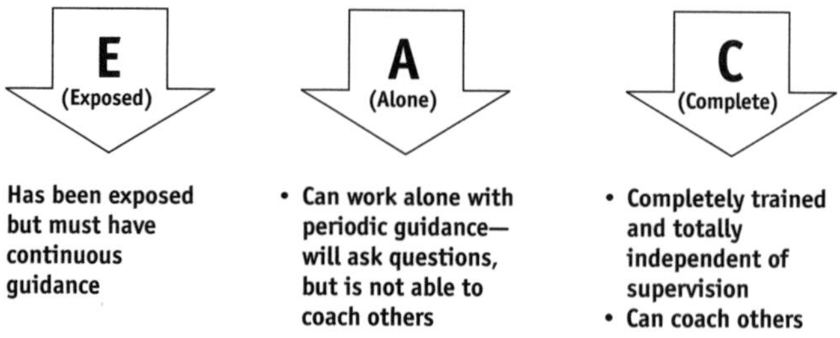

E (Exposed)	**A** (Alone)	**C** (Complete)
• Has been exposed but must have continuous guidance	• Can work alone with periodic guidance—will ask questions, but is not able to coach others	• Completely trained and totally independent of supervision • Can coach others

Figure 9-1. Skill Rating

The marrying of the company's goals with the capabilities of the person is a constant objective, and the ongoing process must allow the individual to work at his or her current level of capability while developing new skills in other areas. As individuals build knowledge and capability, they progress. There are different methods for different situations, but there must be a basic framework for development in order to generate real allowment.

Table 9-1. Skill Sets for a Production Scheduler

	Sub Sets	Description	Elements
Skill Sets — Production activity management	Customer needs analysis	Usage of tools and knowledge in meeting customer requirements	1. Finished goods inventory control list (MIL614) 2. Customer order (COS699)
	Production technology requirements	Knowledge of equipment capabilities, product characteristic knowledge, and transition execution	*Equipment:* RPM CO_2, vacuum, kettle size, packaging, color, blade placement, spec. characteristics *Product knowledge:* color, viscosity, materials, batch sizes, timing *Transition:* flushing, color transitions, material compatibility odor
	Scheduling management	Activities associated with scheduling a manufacturing order to meet a customer ship date	1. Lead-times (Purchasing, routing, mfg., QC) 2. Constraint management (PAC and capacity mgt.) 3. Manufacturing order maintenance
	Timing and yield standards management	Activities that establish and maintain correct labor, machine, and overhead factors that affect labor, yield, and machine variances	1. Manufacturing order maintenance 2. Routing master maintenance 3. Overhead categories by plant/product 4. Formula labor yield update 5. Production yield/hourly report—production variance report
	F.G. inventory development and management	Establishment of required stocking levels and maintenance of those	1. Finished goods listing 2. Buffer stock knowledge 3. EOM inventory valuation (MIL690)
	Non-conforming stock control	Activities that control and utilize non-conforming stock	1. Recook inventory listing (MTL638) 2. Recook balances for mfg. orders (MFG615) 3. Recook activity report by mfg. loc. (MTL678) 4. Rework/brk. stk. inventory listing (MTL662) 5. Manufacturing order maintenance

continued on next page

Table 9-1. Skill Sets for a Production Scheduler (continued)

	Sub Sets	Description	Elements
Production activity management (cont.)	Market specialist communication	Activities performed in order to communicate production status to meet customer order requirements	1. F.G. inventory control list (MTL614) 2. Customer hold maintenance/Customer order inquiry 3. Negotiating skills
Materials management and carrier routing	Materials requirement needs analysis	Those activities that determine what and when to obtain required materials for production	1. Raw materials order action list (MRP606) 2. Raw materials balance inquiry
	Vendor selection process	Methods used to determine proper source of materials, given lead time, pricing, order quantity, freight, and availability of materials to meet production date	1. Raw materials order action list (MRP606) 2. Vendor preference inquiry/Vendor master inquiry 3. Freight inquiry 4. Distribution department contacts
	Materials routing management	Activities that involve establishing pickup, transportation, and delivery of materials	1. Distribution to be routed list (FRT607) 2. Purchase order routing maintenance 3. In-bound carrier list of rates 4. Carrier contacts/Pro number info 5. Warehouse transfer entry/Maintenance 6. Warehouse transfer routing report 7. Bill of lading maintenance
	Purchasing system maintenance and management	Those activities involved with the establishment and maintenance of purchasing parameters, vendor contact and relationship, and purchase order establishment and maintenance	1. Analysis group maintenance/Raw material parameter maintenance 2. Order faxing system/Purchase order maintenance 3. Pickup locations/Pick numbers 4. Freight terms/Routing codes

(Leftmost label: Skill Sets)

Getting to Company Entitlement

Getting to organizational entitlement can be done on a broad basis or within discrete cells identified by management. Within

Table 9-1. Skill Sets for a Production Scheduler (continued)

		Sub Sets	Description	Elements
Skill Sets	**Materials management and carrier routing (cont.)**	Inventory development/ management	Establishment and maintenance of required stocking levels to support production needs in order to meet customer requirements	1. Raw material balance inquiry/Change of classification 2. Buffer stock estab./Raw material transaction history 3. EOM inventory valuation (MTL690)
		COA and vendor defect management	Those activities involved with verifying raw materials quality for usage	1. Vendor lot master maintenance/Vendor defect maintenance 2. Rectification process
	Administrative functions	Process release/ management	Activities related to releasing and updating formulations	1. Manufacturing order release/Manufacturing order maintenance 2. Batch procedure checklist 3. Production schedule
		Administration reports	Those activities involved in the creation and analysis of production reports	1. Variance reports/EOM reports 2. Entitlement reports
		Cost control	Activities performed to control cost of production	1. Production schedule/ Variance reports
		Performance measurements	Knowledge and understanding of plant performance measurements and individual impact	1. Cost of quality 2. Plant performance report (Throughput) 3. Center street expense statement

any number of these cells the process of installing new thoughtware can be done in its entirety.

First, there has to be an understanding of new thoughtware as it relates to the essential components of knowledge, measurement, and velocity. This brings the people up to speed, so to speak, giving them the requisite thoughtware on which to build entitlement. In building their entitlement, people must define their outputs, their authority levels, their skill requirements, and their measurement requirements. The aggregate is a specific and collective definition of allowment.

Table 9-2. Skill Set Matrix for a Manufacturing Supervisor

Required skill sets

	Safety program execution				Performance development and rating				Priority management					Administration functions			
	Program knowledge	System development	Detection and analysis	Program execution	Standards knowledge	Behavior analysis	Measurement methods	Perfm. rating and wage review	Organiz. skills	Resources management	Systems execution	Cost control	People development	Admin. reports	Personnel account. and management	Policy management	Perfm. measure
J. Jones	C	A	A	C	C	A	C	A	A	A	C	A	A	A	C	C	A
S. Smith	A	A	A	A	A	A	A	A	A	A	A	A	A	A	E	A	E
B. Brown	E	A	E	E	E	E	E	E	E	A	E	A	E	A	A	E	A

Additional optional skill sets

	Production activity management				Materials management and carrier routing				Process control development/maintenance					Financial management			
	Customer needs analysis	Production technical requirement	Scheduling management	Mat'l req'd needs analysis	Vendor sel. proc.	Materials routing management	Purch. sys. maintenanc and mgt.	COA and vendor defect. mgt.	Equipment capabilities	Materials knowledge	Methods knowledge	Process development	Process maintenance management	Budget development	Budget management	AFE management	Throughput justification
J. Jones	E	A	A	C	C	C	C	A	A	A	A	C	C	A	A	E	C
S. Smith									C	A	C	E					
B. Brown	E	E	E	C	C	C	C	C									

Next, the people must define their roles and go about getting the information required, developing the needed skills. This is a dynamic process, and each component is not sequentially dependent on the other. Everyone works within the broad framework set out by the new thoughtware; that is, a decentralized, distributed, collaborative, and adaptive cell in which the people are able to do whatever they have to do to get the job done. They set the priorities, allocate the resources, navigate toward the goal, measure results, and are *accountable for outcome.*

This cellular approach to building entitlement can be expanded across the organization at any desired rate, depending on the circumstances, environment, and general state of readiness. It's custom-tailored accordingly. However, within each cell the mandate is for rapid improvement; thus the learning curve for the new thoughtware is sharp and fast. The cellular approach is not a beta test to see how it goes; it's the full-fledged thing, just in a micro-slice that can be repeated over and over until the whole organization is going through a rapid transformation.

Allowment Requires New Learning

Learning is the power of allowment (when I am able, I am allowed), and most of this is new learning, that's obvious. But what may not be so obvious is that the context within which the learning is done is quite different. The new thoughtware automatically changes context, and in so doing creates as much unlearning as new learning.

You don't know what you don't know.

Part of the new context is the self-discipline and self-imposed learning that the people take on. It's no longer an endless parade in and out of the training room trying to absorb a rigorous curriculum of classroom pedagogy; rather, the people lead and learn according to their own requirements as they have defined them (aligned with organizational goals). They are constantly focusing on priorities, accessing information, updating knowledge, and acting at the point of variance. The focus is on experiential and real-time learning (on-the-job or simulation) that directly links the thinking, the action, and new context—where learning and doing are so closely linked that learning becomes an integral part of the individual's work, *not* an add-on.

In *The Fifth Discipline,* Peter Senge talks about the learning disabilities of an organization,[4] and these are quite applicable; however, regardless of what the disabilities are, they cannot be cured until there is a change in the thoughtware on which the learning is based. First new thoughtware, then continuous learning, and then allowment. It's the same as getting the horse before the cart, then the driver in the cart, and then heading off down the road. Historically, we're on the road long before we have all the horses pulling in the right direction or the cart properly built—and then we wonder why the wheels fall off.

Influence Without Authority

As entitlement and allowment take hold, the ability to ignore function and focus on influencing process becomes more and more crucial. It means people must learn how to influence without having or using authority. It's about co-creating, teaming, and leading, because fundamental to leadership is knowing how to influence without authority. It's integral to allowment. Do this, Do that, That's right, That's wrong— such statements are all old thoughtware that no longer fit, no longer work. The new thoughtware of influencing without authority has much more to do with asking the right questions than having the right answers, and this means learning a new set of skills.

Identify Key Variances, Then Allow for Their Most Effective Management

The conversion of input/output processes is complex, and usually includes more complexity than any one manager or employee can deal with. Within these processes there are many variances from what is expected in order to achieve the company's case for action. Identifying these key variances, and getting the right information, skills, and authority in place to minimize them, is what real allowment does. A variance analysis is the starting point in transferring the required information, skills, and authority. The analysis identifies a range of issues, as listed below:

Variance Control Analysis
- The key variance
- Where it occurs
- Where it's observed
- Where it's controlled
- Who controls it
- Activities required to control it
- Information required to control it
- Suggestions for redesign, reconfiguration
- Suggestions for changes in technology
- Suggested skill requirements
- Suggested authority requirements

The analysis is part of the technical changes required to reach allowment, but far more important are the changes required in the social side of the business: understanding and accepting the power of allowment.

The power of allowment is anchored in the organization's value system. First the values must be there. Second, they must be perpetuated and propagated throughout the organization so that they become self-evident. If the goal is to deliver real value to the customer, for which the organization receives fair value in return, then the value of the employees must be understood, invested in, and allowed to grow. It only comes when the organization exudes trust, fairness, and integrity; recognizes individual capability; and provides both the means *and* the opportunity for growth. In turn, the individual must be committed to his or her role, have or acquire the necessary knowledge and skills, and perform at the required level of capability. From this, allowment flourishes and creates a powerful, fast, flexible, focused organization, moving to the future with an unprecedented level of capability and unlimited potential.

Notes

[1] C. William Pollard, *The Soul of the Firm* (New York: Harper Business, 1996).

[2] Keith Hammonds, "Balancing Work and Family," *Business Week,* September 16, 1996, p. 74.

[3] Ibid, p. 74.

[4] Peter Senge, *The Fifth Discipline* (New York: Doubleday, 1990).

PART THREE

installation

Enactment

10

You think you understand the situation, but what you don't understand is that the situation just changed.

The collective thinking of people and their interactions determines the nature of an organization, how it performs, and ultimately what it will be. This collective thoughtware constantly generates action, movement. Historically, however, we have found that we have a propensity to analyze and plan, and *then* act. But this method seldom delivers the needed results. Why? Edward de Bono points out that it is because so much is logical in hindsight, and this knowledge engenders constant analysis in hot pursuit of ready answers. Instead of looking behind ourselves, however, we need to design our way *forward*—to ask questions, not formulate answers, to leave *what is* where it is so we can unearth new discoveries with new thinking. In this chapter, we'll begin to create a strategy for looking forward, to enacting the new thoughtware.

Answers: A mechanism for avoiding questions.

—JOHN RALSTON SAUL

Thinking Is an Action—You Are What You Think

A sequential mentality breeds a permanent case of anxiety between planning and action. We either overplan or jump into action, but we never find the middle ground. Guess what? There is no middle ground. We think of planning as being a cerebral function separate from implementation, where thinking and planning come first, and only then—when the thinking is done—does the action begin. New thoughtware counters this: It proffers that *thinking is an action.* There is no middle ground between planning and action; they're synonymous. Strategic planning can and should be an action, not a function, a verb, not a noun. You may think things you don't do, but you never do things you don't think. *You are what you think.*

We tend to isolate thinking and set out plans and strategies as something to ponder for a period of time, and then act upon some other time (which could be hours or months after the thinking has occurred). This old thoughtware simply does not reflect the way things are. Indeed, some of the most successful companies in the world have been built by entrepreneurs who seldom, if ever, put their strategic thinking into a plan first. Because they constantly live their strategic thinking, there is no time to plan before acting. Their thinking, planning, strategy, and action are simultaneous and continuously play off each other. This is not a sequential or linear process; this is a continuous process of thinking.

Most, if not all, implementation models currently in vogue cannot adequately address or respond to today's demands for change. Change is not some fast-approaching, rolling mass that we can build a model for and gear up to meet. It is here. It is constant. It demands instant response, every day. There is no time to ponder change, to plan change, to ask if we should change this or that. We must be capable of changing continuously, without laborious planning, without bureaucratic decision making, without oppressive structure. To do this, *thinking and action must be synonymous and integral at the point of change*. Then, and only then, does implementation move from being a mechanistic model aimed at solving problems to *a natural and continuous response* that dissolves problems before, or as, they occur.

Implementation Has to Be Collective Thoughtware in Action

We cannot reduce implementation to a formal, step-by-step process (that invariably creates precisely the opposite of what we need). The context in which we work is much too dynamic for that, and so is the required thoughtware. It's a complex combination of philosophy, thinking, relationships, information, techniques, and action. The new thoughtware cannot be seen as another new and improved technique; rather, it must become *collective thinking in action that is rooted in a transcendent philosophy*. Reengineering was seen primarily as a technique without a solidly based philosophy, consequently, it became little more than an exercise in downsizing. TQM has been a wonderful philosophy with the new thoughtware imbedded in its assumptions, but it has lacked technique—

especially in its early years. Only when the thinking is in balance and synonymous with the techniques and the action can we have effective implementation.

Time to Implementation Is a Drag

In the new thoughtware time is recognized as one of the most highly valued resources. It realizes that time is a resource and money a metric; whereas old thoughtware sees money as the resource and time as the metric. Today, to optimize money (profits), we must economize time (the resource), and nowhere is this more applicable than in the time span between planning and implementation, between production and sale, between concept and consumption. Ultimately, the goal is to fulfill demand as it occurs—instantly.

> *If you're in a vehicle traveling at the speed of light,*
> *what happens when you turn on your headlights?*

Time is where an exorbitant amount of costs are tied up, but it hasn't always been that way. In the agricultural era, time was not an important factor in production, as it did not dramatically affect costs. In the industrial era, time was a larger part of costs and mass production helped reduce some of those costs. However, today, in the knowledge era, response time is one of the most influential factors in performance. It is the primary variable in product development, one of a company's most important strategic weapons. Time is the most effective focus for process improvement; it is the least threatening, most accessible, and offers a common language for everyone to use.

If your organization is changing at the
speed of change, what happens?
Smooth, relevant, immediate change.

As the new "operational optic" that holds process elements constant, measuring time reduction allows data to be collected so that it translates directly into cash returns. Design and production can become simultaneous (as in software development or customer-designed greeting cards), and mass customization is no longer an oxymoron. We have become a minimal time-lag world: the Internet, ATMs, CNN, Federal Express. With things moving at the speed of light, we have to rid ourselves of the lag time between past and future by turning thinking into action on a dime (or it'll cost us a dollar).

What Is EnACTment?

Because the organization is the critical vehicle for getting to the future, it must not tie up excessive amounts of time between planning and implementation. We need to create a context in which thinking, planning, and action coexist, interact, thrive, and concurrently drive the organization—where there is no lag time between past and future. We call this *EnACTment*. Enactment engages thinking, planning, and action. It brings them together and decrees that no longer can one be considered without the other. The focus is not only on shortening or eliminating the gap between thinking, planning, and action, but also on creating a new context in which all three components interact. Old thoughtware implementers see action flowing from strategy, but new thoughtware enactors see the reverse: In this mode, the organization is not pulled along by strategy; rather, the organization continuously pushes strategy to realization—it constantly *enacts*.

Effective enactment is the result of a unique blend of philosophy and technique. It does not evolve simply by applying proven techniques and tools. Instead, it requires a founding philosophy (the new thoughtware) that provides the right context in which the techniques can work. The new thoughtware takes into full consideration the changing context (e.g., knowledge and information), the importance of the socioeconomic aspects of the organization (relationships), and the enormous investment a company has in its human assets (human capital). All are essential elements in building a future capability, today.

When new thoughtware is a dynamic, daily process— a part of the philosophy that proliferates every facet of the organization—then the techniques, tools, and programs of change are optimized. No longer is planning waiting in limbo for implementation to begin or implementation waiting for planning to be completed. They are one. We have enactment.

Removing Stop Signs

Often what stops people from changing is their own vested interest in creating a secure place for themselves, a place where they have a stake in keeping the problem identified but *not* resolved. As previously mentioned, they often have a fear of the change process itself, whereby they agree with the goal of change but fear the process of getting there. These stop signs keep many organizations mired in the status quo. Until these barricades are dismantled, there can be no enactment. However, as we expose old thoughtware and develop new thoughtware, we begin to interact differently and deal with things beyond the problem, beyond the barricade. As a group, we leave the problem where it is and undertake new and often quite different action. As we change our thinking, we have no choice but to move in a new direction, because we know the old way—the old thoughtware—is obsolete. We've removed the stop signs and there's no going back. The thinking has changed and the organization's behavior is changing with it.

Building New Communication Vehicles

We can't change everyone's thinking, that's clear. But we don't have to if we can create a process that *generates* new thinking and install a discipline (a methodology) that constantly *breeds* new thinking on which the organization runs. In other words, while we can't implement new thoughtware, we can install a methodology that *produces* new thoughtware.

Change happens through the network of interactions in the organization, not through the hierarchy. Only when you build processes that link horizontally can real change occur and become part of everyday operations. You cannot significantly change an organization vertically, yet so many of the communication vehicles we have employed over the years, such as job descriptions and performance reviews, are vertical, top down. None of these communication vehicles are horizontal. Therefore they have little impact.

As in most things, you need champions of new thoughtware who understand and demonstrate it on the level of their own actions, so that it eventually permeates the organization—people who carry the understanding until the rest get it. Pockets will emerge here and there in the organization as people begin to get hold of the new thinking and how to act on it.

At the Center for Creative Learning in Palo Alto, California, they use the term "meaning making," which aptly describes this process. As it spreads, resources will be reallocated, priorities will change, new scorecards will emerge. People must learn how to manage from the future, as if the future were here, and manage all actions toward that end. This thinking has a dimension and rigor that replaces any linear, step-by-step implementation process. This is not a one-time event, but an ongoing exercise in new understanding and the incorporation of enabling tools that support action.

Thoughtware doesn't set out to directly change everyone's thinking, *it simply creates a platform on which only new thinking works,* thus allowing new thinking to be the constant modus operandi. Old thinking becomes non-essential, non-contributory, not profitable, and eventually disappears.

The new thoughtware must be installed through the network of relationships throughout the organization. There are enabling technologies like intranet e-mail, Lotus notes, and Domino, but it is the thoughtware that supports these networks of information, these structural capital pieces as we refer to them, that really becomes the raison d'être of that organization. Bill Gates didn't change his organization, in fact, he was headed on a different track altogether. Microsoft's changes really came from deep within the organization, from new thinking that was allowed to grow because of the type of thoughtware embedded in the organization. Honda's CEO, Nobuhiko Kawamoto, instilled a new attitude whereby "the trend is toward getting back together so we can share ideas and fix problems more quickly" and away from old ways where the "thinking became vague."[1] He was out to install new thoughtware to create new thinking.

IBM faced a similar challenge in 1985, but its top management stuck with its old, linear thinking: Although the people in the trenches were communicating over and over again, "We are getting killed in the PC market," top management concluded that if a computer didn't have the IBM logo nobody was going to buy it. To them, in 1985 at least, the idea of a clone PC was bizarre—especially to a company that owned 98 percent of the PC market. So they couldn't see the critical importance of negotiating proprietary rights to Bill Gates' disk operating system (DOS). The same blindness occurred with Intel's microprocessing chip. Only after IBM was left behind by Microsoft and Intel did they declare the computer a commodity. By 1988, IBM was bleeding to death and everybody else was building computers, but top management still said, "Don't worry, nobody will buy the competition's computers because they won't plug into our mainframes." Once again, they completely missed what was going on. The moral? The logic of where you are going is only logical in hindsight, but it is not logic that gets you there. You must be flexible enough to be constantly tripping over opportunities and seeing them and responding to them.

A Coalition of Thought

Enactment does not automatically happen. Before an organization can install new thoughtware on a comprehensive basis *there must be a core group of committed new thinkers—a coalition of thought—who develop the platform for new thoughtware and initiate the transformation throughout the organization.* This group, usually a senior management group, must ensure that the organization can meet the criteria for installing new thoughtware, and that the organization is entitled (ready and capable) to allow major change to take place. This coalition of thought does not have to be a massive movement (not yet anyway); it only needs to be a well-founded force of thinking, a few people who can articulate and hold the new thoughtware vision constant until others get it. It becomes a launching platform.

But a coalition of thought is not enough to generate enduring change. It takes critical mass to do this, and achieving critical mass requires the new coalition to communicate and act the new thoughtware philosophy *and* the techniques that can unlock and link the complexities of an ever-changing organization. In the following chapters we'll talk more about the framework for installing integrated, new thoughtware—philosophy and techniques that create the needed coalition and catalyze critical mass. In the meantime, let's continue looking at the pieces that need to be in place for enactment to occur.

Asking the Right Questions

> *If the only tool you have is a chain saw,*
> *everything begins to look like a tree*
> *(and you can't see the forest for the trees).*

The early coalition of thought, in its enthusiasm to install new thoughtware, quite often encounters its first stumbling block: the group cannot agree on what enactment looks like. It's reminiscent of the story of Winnie the Pooh and his friends hunting for a Heffalump. They think they should dig a hole to catch the Heffalump but they don't know what a

Heffalump looks like so they don't know how deep to dig the hole. They don't know where to find a Heffalump so they don't know where to dig the hole. And they don't know what a Heffalump eats so they don't know what food to put in the hole. Needless to say, Winnie and Tigger and Piglet never catch a Heffalump. Our moral to the story: Before hunting for enactment, you must understand what it looks like, what it is, and what it is not.

This process starts with the coalition of thought realizing that the thinking, planning, and action must be totally integrated and fully in sync. The organization is not ready until this occurs. Then, and only then, can there be an understanding of what enactment is (a well-defined Heffalump)—coming from the same new thoughtware, moving in the same direction, with the same purpose, and generating consistent action. This is wholly integrated thinking.

> *It is far worse to have the right answer*
> *to the wrong question than to have*
> *the wrong answer to the right question.*

There are several ways to begin installing new thoughtware, but first new thoughtware requires the rigorous application of several crucial questions. The answers to these questions are the footings in the foundation of the new thoughtware platform. The answers to these questions give you an intuitive check as to which is greater, the barriers or the catalysts to change.

1. Do you accept that many current support structures are obsolete?
2. Do you focus on process rather than techniques?

3. Does your organization entirely revolve around the customer?

4. Do your measurements provide navigational information?

5. Do you view and measure people as valued-added assets?

6. Do you quantify intellectual capital (on the balance sheet)?

7. Do you understand how technology drives organizational structure?

8. Do you subscribe to creating a lifelong learning organization?

The answers to these questions should be yes. But the question behind these questions is Do you believe that you are ready and able to get to the yes—to enact?

A Platform for New Thoughtware

It is very important not to rush the new process until the philosophy of thoughtware is solidly installed; however, it does not have to be a long transition. Once the fundamentals are understood, enactment and the ongoing installment of new thoughtware can go hand in hand. New thoughtware, and dramatic change, can spread like wildfire just as soon as the philosophy is ingrained at the senior levels. But, be aware that there is no neat, detailed, cut-and-dried model that you can take off the shelf to begin installing new thoughtware—it is much too robust for that. On the other hand, the philosophy is easily integrated with custom-tailored techniques to create an overarching *thoughtware methodology* that provides a tangible, concrete, and straightforward way of dramatically changing the organization without trashing all that has gone before. And in so doing, it places the collective mind-set and perception of the organization *in the future* now, creating the all-important new context needed to understand and get to the future.

The transformation can be far-reaching, but to get there the organization must have the capability to transform new thinking into a platform of new thoughtware. This means a vehicle is needed for installing new thoughtware. It is much more of a grass roots operation than a top-down engagement. The top-down declares the *what* but not the *how*. Enactment is not a step-by-step installation, nor can you install thoughtware in a classroom. I could sit here and say I think I am going to learn to play the piano, and I could learn music theory, but until I sit down and play, it cannot be called *playing the piano*. Thoughtware is like this. It is not just theory or problem solving, it is learning to design a way forward. It is constantly exploring a myriad of alternatives. It is giving everybody in the organization permission to participate. But don't let this approach fool you into thinking this is simple to do. There is an enormous amount of discipline in thoughtware's framework— and, like playing the piano, there are some non-negotiable discipline points that you can't ignore.

Thus far, we have described the old thoughtware—division of labor, departmentalization, span of control, and point of authority—and the new—knowledge, measurement, time to action, and allowment. We have also set out some specific requirements in order for your organization to cross over from old thoughtware to new. Every organization's circumstances, needs, position in time, and old thoughtware are different, and there is no off-the-shelf panacea; however, there are universal, key components that constitute a blueprint for designing and constructing a new means to the end—*your* end, *your* goals, *your* needs. In the following chapters we describe the components of the blueprint and the tools you will need for installing the new thoughtware. We also address the problems, issues, and processes you may encounter. The vehicle you will build is one that can drive the entire organization into the future. It is by its very nature fast, flexible, and focused. It allows self-steering, self-righting, can spin on a dime, out-maneuver competition, and withstand extreme conditions. It cannot leap tall buildings in a single bound, but it can destroy silos and barriers and eliminate large warehouses. The vehicle acts like a master navigational system, constantly setting priorities, allocating resources, and changing actions— all in direct response to new context, the changing environment, and the rapidly forming future. It's at the center of the operations, enabling the organization to change at will. Let's look at how to put it together.

Notes

[1] "On Track," *Fortune,* September 9, 1996. p. 94.

A Vehicle for Installing the New Thoughtware

11

The actions of men are the best interpreters of their thoughts.

—John Locke

We Can't Get There Without a Vehicle

All the philosophy in the world will not change the world until it has a means to do so. Such is the case with contextual change and the installation of new thoughtware. A methodology, a vehicle, designed specifically to facilitate installation is needed, and an understanding of such a methodology is essential in the transformation to a new organization. Let's look at the installation process.

An Evolution Plan: The Engine

Even though we recommend initially building "a plan," the secret is in the process of building it, not in the plan itself. The purpose of the evolution plan is *to create a new process with new thoughtware*. This is not planning in the traditional sense.

This is not a plan built by a few, executed by many, and jammed into an organization for which it does not fit. Quite the opposite. This is a plan designed by many, for many, from which a new organization evolves. Parts of the process and some of the initial outputs are familiar, but what *is* different is a process that engenders a collective vision—a common purpose, with real ownership and commitment all imbedded in the new thoughtware. The evolution plan becomes the central manifestation of how the organization designs itself forward.

One of the main reasons for first developing a plan is that it provides a focus to which people are accustomed, and allows them to cross over from old to new thoughtware. But what really counts is the process of getting there. For it is the process of building the plan that generates new discipline, spawns new thoughtware, and builds a bridge into new context. The process eventually manifests itself in new thinking and becomes "the way we do business."

The evolution plan is tactical, not strategic; therefore, although we begin by building a plan, we end up leaving it behind. Once the plan is complete, the organization leaves it where it is and moves on to continuously create and re-create—through the now entrenched process—whatever is necessary to respond to constantly shifting demands. The blueprint thinking in this book does not lay out all the "specs" and "how to's" of creating the evolution plan. Only your organization can do that, within the context of *your* business. What we have set out is the foundation, the footings, and the framing of new thoughtware that provides the two fundamental requirements to move ahead: (1) an evolution plan and (2) a new process. Some pieces will sound familiar (strategic intent, case for action, cross-functionality, process thinking, and so on), but the differences lie in the new thoughtware on which they are built.

We have set out in this chapter the general framework within which the evolution planning is done, and shown *how the process of installing new thoughtware creates ongoing, sustainable change.*

We repeat, thoughtware cannot be implemented. It's not a program that is here today, gone tomorrow. New thoughtware can only be installed, allowing you to create a new platform in which the organization operates and in which continuous enactment takes place. Thoughtware is always here, always driving, forming, directing, or misdirecting the organization. The real issue is making sure that the organization has the right thoughtware, and, if it's running on old thoughtware, knowing how to initiate the installation of new thoughtware. The end result is a dramatically new, and different, management process for adapting to change.

Installation of new thoughtware at no time usurps the reality of the requisite hierarchy of the organization—the boss is the boss, and he or she cannot renege on accountability. However, what can be done is to establish a top-level, fully cross-functional team that sets out the organization's strategic intent and case for action (outlined later in this chapter), from which grows a new evolutionary process, built on new thoughtware. When the senior management team gets the strategic intent and case for action right and in place, the rest follows, cascading down through the organization (see Figure 11-3).

A Framework for Installation

Installing new thoughtware can be done in more than one way, as long as the fundamentals and principles remain hard and fast. How to rebuild an organization with new thoughtware does not come shrink-wrapped on three or four disks—sorry, this is thoughtware, not software. For thoughtware, each organization is its own programmer, and the installation must be custom-tailored. The first requirement is an understanding of the basic installation process. We have graphically depicted the overall process with the use of a series of illustrations.

Figure 11-1 shows the major elements and overall flow of the installation process. The planning process leads to the creation of the evolution plan. The management process is separate from, but provides parallel support to, the planning process. The support systems provide an ongoing framework for all processes. The evolution plan is a result of the initial planning process, but thereafter becomes a continuous discipline or process by which the organization manages the way it does business. Enactment (implementation) becomes a continuous, responsive process driving the business.

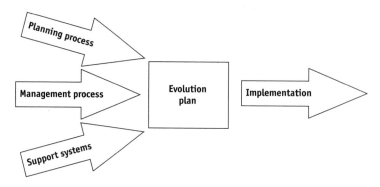

Figure 11-1. The Overall Installation Process

Figure 11-2 is the continuous-flow installation of the key components of new thoughtware. It begins with knowledge of the whole, moves to measurement of what matters (tools for navigation), then to a focus on time to action, and then to

allowment (distributed authority). The internal arrows indicate
the direction of growth in that element of the thoughtware: you
want measurement or motivation to go up, knowledge of the
whole to go up, point of authority to push down by means of
allowment, and time to action to decrease.

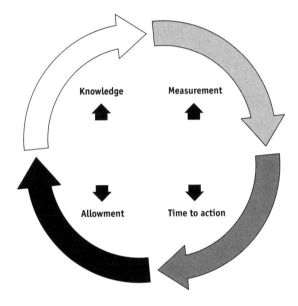

Figure 11-2. Installing New Thoughtware Components

Figure 11-3 represents the transformation from the current
traditional management process to the new evolutionary management process. The installation cascades top-down from
vision and strategy and the case for action to an evolution plan
and its implementation, and at each stage the key components
of new thoughtware are installed. By the third stage (third
circle) a critical mass of the organization is operating with new
thoughtware and integrated implementation is well underway.
(We will refer back to these figures as we describe the eight
modules of installation in Chapter 12.)

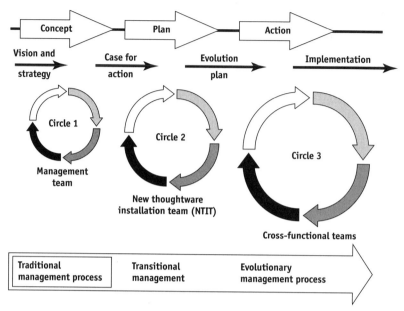

Figure 11-3. Cascading the Installation (Three Phases)

Circle One

This first stage answers "what." Management clearly defines what outcomes they expect. There must be a continuous flow of installation of the key components of the new thoughtware. To install a horizontal process where a vertical one exists, you have to start at the top of the pyramid with the executive committee, because they call the shots. But all you need from them is an articulation of what they want—a clarification of what success looks like at the end of the day. An example would be a goal of reducing cycle time in half. All the players who impact cycle time will be given this as part of the case for action to create a game plan to achieve the required result—half of today's cycle time.

Circle Two

This second stage answers "how." How will the organization get there and how will it know if it's moving in the right direction? The new thoughtware installation team goes away to create the evolution plan for achieving cycle time reduction. In the planning process people must learn how to build relationship maps, cross-functional maps, and a navigational measurement system, as well as apply cost-time profiling. These enabling tools allow them to come back with different answers to the questions posed in the case for action. Meanwhile the management team is learning how to manage the evolution plan that will be coming back to them for approval.

Circle Three

This third stage answers "the doing." It's either rapid deployment or longer-horizon framework building (i.e., new compensation), or held in inventory until it becomes a higher priority. In the third circle, you release the evolution plan into the environment for implementation by the cross-functional operational teams. The management team determines which projects to release first. Everything recommended in the evolution plan cannot be implemented at once, so setting priorities and allocating resources will be the critical factor to ensure success. The other thing that's important about the third circle is that you distinguish between the "what" and the "how." Those teams are executing the how but not the what. If they get involved with the what, most teams become dysfunctional because they spend most of the time spinning their wheels trying to decide on the what. Any "what" discussion is dysfunctional conflict. A "how" discussion is functional conflict. Functional conflict creates progress.

The Interactive Process

This is an interactive process embedded in the three outputs—the case for action, the evolution plan, and the enactment. It must be disciplined and nutured completely and continuously, often taking seven or eight months, until the management team takes ownership through the *daily habit* of doing it. You keep moving through the three cycles of concept, plan, and action until they are all functioning simultaneously. After that, the evolution plan and installation teams are no longer needed. The process is in full play, and it will now occur naturally. Teams now come together and are released to implement what is prioritized (you can close the door and slide pizza under the door until they're finished), and then they reorganize and do it again for another requirement in the case for action. This allows the organization to move on a dime, with everyone moving in the same direction, with the same information, and supported by the same advocation system.

An important factor in the interactive process is to make it digestible, in bite-size pieces that allow success on the first try. It would be inappropriate to ask a team to put in a completely new computer logistics system. It's better to ask them to install and deploy a synchronous flow system that can be broken into a series of cells and then tied together. That kind of deployment will be successful and will make them want to do it again and again and again.

Support Systems

Inherent in the process are support systems. They are usually released in the midst of the process (see Figure 11-1). If, for example, you put in three distinct cycle time systems on the floor and plug them together, you may find you need a new costing system. You might need a new pay system on the floor so that you are paying people for flexibility. You might need a new measurement system. You need to add new systems until you have a structure in place that sustains the new thoughtware. In other words, during the planning and action phases, and while the new thoughtware is wheeling throughout the organization, there is also training and application of process improvement tools and other enabling systems. Some of the support systems will be part of the initial evolution plan, and some will emerge as everything cascades into the organization. As it expands, the organization will indicate what is required to support the changes being made.

This internal momentum will begin to occur about three or four months into the installation period. For example, demands from one installation team may come in to change the way the beans are counted. They recommend a plan to introduce an activity-based costing model and it goes into the bin of projects to be considered for resource allocation. Then it is weighed against all the other demands and against the available resources, and finally moves ahead based on overall priorities.

When you reach the point at which a critical mass of installed new thoughtware is actually functioning as the decider of priorities, you will have reached a point where the evolution plan is operating in a new context that is oriented toward flexible response to customer demand. For instance, the evolution plan may be about changing the entire Microsoft organization to take advantage of the Internet, but somewhere, long before that, there was thoughtware installed in the organization that allowed the conflict and questions—the new thinking—about the direction Gates was going, to be challenged, debated, and changed. Then, the whole thing shifted to a new strategic intent.

Where to Start?

The best way out is always through.
— ROBERT FROST

Start with flexibility. Flexibility is being able to respond as far downstream in the process as possible. Flexibility is an operational definition. It is not efficiency. In fact, it is the anti-thesis of efficiency in many cases. For example, at a call center for a nationwide retail organization, hundreds of people are learning to respond to any type of customer inquiry you can imagine, rather than having to bump the caller from one operator to another depending on the question. That is flexibility at the point of variance as far downstream as possible—right at the customer interface. That is flexibility in an operational sense. In the case of Microsoft, what Bill Gates *did* do, and was *able* to do, was be flexible in a strategic sense. But it is the installed thoughtware that allows this kind of flexibility—or prevents it.

A company in Milwaukee is working to get to a place it has never been before—from a commodity transaction manufacturer to a business-solution business. Instead of making glue, they are building laminations, subassemblies, a completely different understanding of their purpose and product. They have the capabilities and flexibility to respond to this challenge now. A sign of a very healthy business is the ability to tremendously reduce concept-to-commercialization cycles. McDonald's puts up 3,000 new stores a year. How do they do it so fast?

Eventually you must change the way you score the business, the way you measure it, the way you compensate it, the way you motivate it. It requires a redesign of the whole social fabric, not just the technical side. Returning to the example of the call center, operators are being encouraged to log and categorize every call into the system, so they have a database of their experience to draw upon the next time a similar call comes in. This is different behavior. You don't have to put in a program to get people to do this, you have to put in a *framework for people to understand that this is important to do*—a framework that will get them to think differently. Of course, you must also pay them for the increased knowledge that they accumulate.

Often you will hear managers say, "Oh yeah, we understand what you're talking about. We're leading-edge people," and so on, and then you challenge them to pay for knowledge and show them how a pay-for-knowledge system works. Invariably we hear, "We only want to pay our people for *demonstrated* knowledge." In other words, to pay them for what they do, not for what they know. Demonstrated knowledge is just a euphemism for the same old idea. There is no intuitive recognition or confidence in the fact that as people learn more, they are going to be more productive, that customer retention rates will go through the roof if all of these people have all of these capabilities. These "leading edge" managers can't be flexible enough to make the needed leap. They can talk about a knowledge-based pay system, but they can't enact it because they don't really understand it. *The thoughtware is not there.* Instead they perceive paying for knowledge to be too high risk. What if this person gains all of this knowledge and they don't get any more productive? If you have to ask this question then you are still cruising back in the good old days of old thoughtware.

A big barrier to flexibility is too many egos blocking the way. The idea is to get the ego out of the way and look at the situation objectively, as a team. This is what is powerful about new thoughtware—it removes egos and allows people to deliberately think and to objectively look at the situation, and to listen deep within the organization and discover your sustaining competitive advantage.

When critical mass is reached, the organization now *is* the information and knowledge being communicated. The idea that strategy leads action blinds you to flexibility. Strategy is simply the formal articulation of what is already so, and the *thoughtware* leads the organization to where it is already going. The task of leadership is to listen to the thoughtware and put the resources in the right place to take the organization in the direction new thoughtware is leading. Predicting the future is almost impossible. The best thing you can do given the turbulence of today's environment is to redeploy your resources to be flexible enough to respond faster than the next guy to whatever changes happen. That's a better strategy than trying to forecast the changes. But nine out of ten businesses out there are building their whole logistics systems on the weakest component—the forecast—which is really, when you think about it, rather silly. If you try to forecast what is going to happen and build systems around it, it *might not happen*. It makes more sense if you can get closer to making a decision at the final point downstream. Here you are in a better position to know the score.

An example of downstream thinking is manifested in the concept of outsourcing, whereby certain capabilities are put to a cost-benefit analysis and then outsourced or not. Hewlett-Packard will have a logistics company do their testing, their assembly, and their shipment. They'll build components, somebody will phone the logistics company and say I want this configuration, and they'll configure it and get it out in 24 hours because they've got a mass of logistics trucking capabilities, which Hewlett-Packard doesn't. But now Hewlett-Packard has the ability to focus on what it is good at: building components and becoming, as much as possible, totally flexible to customer demand—whatever you order you can have now. At Dell, for instance, they will put exactly the software you want on your computer and ship it in 24 hours. That's flexible.

Moving out of old context into a new context is best achieved by going out through one, or all, of the current windows of opportunity—the elements of the old thoughtware (e.g., division of labor, and so forth)—for each leads to the construct of a vital vehicle for change. We can enter anywhere, depending on the need and situation. For example, if there is a preponderance of issues stuck in the old thoughtware of *division of labor,* then start there, and get at the core truth of process thinking. This involves the application of cross-functionality by gathering together people to discuss relationships, customer requirements, and process flow. This will create new thoughtware and *knowledge of the whole.* From this will come new action. The same approach applies individually, or collectively, to the other windows of thoughtware, i.e., from departmentalization to horizontalism and measurement of what matters, from span of control to focus on time to action, from point of authority to allowment and distributed points of authority. But, before getting to these we must complete four, non-negotiable prerequisites that are the underpinnings of successful installation.

Prerequisite One: Commitment Through Ownership

First, we must separate the *builders* of the plan from the *approvers* of the plan. This is a crucial demarcation because it leads to permanent role changes that move people out of old context. It allows grassroots involvement, separates the "what" from the "how," strips away bureaucracy, encourages initiative, unbridles creativity, and builds commitment. Most importantly, it makes the *builders* and the *doers* of the plan one and the same (while separating the approvers). The builders and doers own the plan. It becomes their commitment, their mandate, and a stake-in-the-ground for their motivation. This process also helps deliver to the organization complete commitment as opposed to partial commitment. We are reminded of that infamous comment by Henry Ford when he asked, "Why is it that I always get the whole person, when what I really want is a pair of hands?"[1] Henry didn't get it. People were not just another mindless cog on the assembly line then—and they certainly aren't today. Obviously, commitment is imperative in building any viable team, and commitment results from having *meaningful purpose*.

Sometimes, this separation of the builders/doers from approvers is an uncomfortable leap, and when it is, business simulation (which is a risk-free environment) can play an important part in understanding the process and outcomes, and allaying fear of taking risks. Regardless of how you handle this separation, it is a fundamental first step in eventually getting the commitment and the involvement of the whole organization.

Prerequisite Two: Strategic Intent

The organization cannot wade into this new territory without some essential, up-front pieces in place. Before setting out to build the evolution plan there must be a clear connection between the organization's strategic intent and the plan. If there already is a clear strategic intent, then review it, reconfirm it, and recommunicate it. *If there isn't one, get one,* because strategic intent creates both the starting point and the horizon of your evolution plan.

Strategic intent is not strategy. Strategy is definitive, directional, and explicit. Strategic intent is the challenge from which strategy emanated. As Gary Hamel and C. K. Prahalad say in their book, *Competing for the Future,* we should think of strategy as "the brain" of the organization and strategic intent as "the heart." This heart carries the emotion, the energy, and the belief. It is the emotional conversion of the "we can do it" aspiration and the goal that allows everyone to embrace strategy. Strategic intent is not limited by resources or constrained by feasibility studies. It reaches beyond these restraints and projects the destiny of the organization. It is the clear description of the organization's key purposes, the anchor point from which new thoughtware evolves and to which all thinking should relate. For it to do this it must be well founded and well grounded in such key principles as what need the organization is going to fulfill, who the organization wants to serve, how it will accomplish its goals, the core competencies around which it will focus, what direction it must take, and what it intends to return to its stakeholders.

Your strategic intent needs to set a beyond-the-grasp challenge that demands to be fulfilled. If you build it, they will come. Coca-Cola's intent is to have a Coke within arm's reach of everyone in the world. Kamatsu (the Japanese competitor to Caterpillar) has said they want to engulf Caterpillar. These are beyond-the-horizon, challenging strategic intents. If the organizational thinking (all of it, not just the senior people) isn't out on this trajectory, then you are destined to always be stuck in the gantry, sitting on the launching pad.

Prerequisite Three: A Case for Action

What must quickly come into focus is the future. Strategic intent, which is founded in the future, *must be operationalized* so as to set direction, time-bound objectives, quantifiable tasks, and relevant measures—for *all* to understand. It must be put forward as a case for action, a specific statement of what the organization expects to achieve in pursuit of its greater purpose. Once the future is well defined, then strategy becomes operational, and strategy and action are inextricably linked. Only then can the organization respond in full force.

First, senior management must be intimate with the strategic intent which qualifies them to put forward a case for action—and they had better not do it with old thoughtware, or the organization will be going in the wrong direction, or treading water trying to find direction. The case for action is a definitive declaration of direction and goals, married to the strategic intent. It is developed by a full cross-functional representation of senior management, and literally sets the agenda for the business. It puts before "the jury" the strongest possible case for where the organization is going, and why.

The case for action becomes recalibration; it tells the organization what, and what not, to do. It is not about piling more work on top of existing work; it's about smart management identifying the things they think the organization should be putting its resources into that will give it the greatest return and momentum toward its future. And it's deciding this collectively as part of the thoughtware system. This acting together dramatically increases the probability that not only will you enact the right things, you will also stop doing 60 or 70 percent of the stupid things you are doing now that you don't need to do. The case for action lets you know that some fires are meant to burn. Let them burn. This is a process of regeneration. Prioritize, allocate resources—that is the task. This is what the process is about—priority, not capacity. Management can leverage the organization in three ways:

1. Recognize that capacity is a function of reliability, dependability, and flexibility; therefore anything that affects those dimensions is an opportunity.
2. Understand that leverage for action increases directly in relation to how many people are using process improvement tools and other enabling support tools throughout the organization. As more people use the same information and move in the same direction, you can focus more on training, allowing, and distributing the authority to act.
3. Make it your primary role to continually shift priorities and reallocate resources wherever and whenever you recognize the demand has shifted.

The case for action must be something that allows everyone to buy in. It requires understanding—initially at the senior levels, and then throughout the organization—about where you are and where you are going. In formulating a case for action there must be a clear understanding *by all senior managers* of (1) the imperative of new context, (2) the dramatic difference between old and new thoughtware, (3) the critical relationship between change philosophy and change techniques, and (4) how the business process, *as a whole,* works. These are important cornerstones for developing new thoughtware, and getting started starts with senior management getting them. "Only senior managers can rise above the details of the business, recognize emerging patterns, make unexpected connections, and identify the points of maximum leverage for action."[2]

Today, in many organizations, the greatest leverage on which to build a case for action is the operating imperative of *time* (versus the other two imperatives of cost and quality). Quality is a given, and in most cases traditional costs are already well in hand; therefore, time offers by far the greatest leverage and access. This provides an unmatched opportunity to focus on many of the major drivers or deterrents of the business, and to develop a quantification *in time* of the organization's case for action. Remember, time provides an operational optic that is accessible to everyone.

A Few Parameters for a Case for Action
- Cycle time from receipt of order to delivery from 120 days to under 30 days
- 75 percent reduction in non-value-added activity
- 75 percent reduction in paperwork
- Design all products to be modular in concept
- Create continuous flow for all information and parts processes
- Full access to all required information
- Complete information, documentation, and design prior to building
- Abandon rates under 3 percent
- Call-transfer-time reduction
- Queue-time reduction
- As much customer participation as possible

It doesn't matter what the parameters are as long as they are clear, concise, and leverage off of reliability, dependability, and capability.

The case for action doesn't just fall from on high—it doesn't just happen. As mentioned, senior management must be thoroughly versed in the strategic intent and understand the fundamentals of new thoughtware before setting out the case for action. This happens in the first two modules of installation. See Chapter 12.

Prerequisite Four: New Roles Are a Must

Now that the "what" is defined and the "how" has been handed over, management must address its new role. Changing the way the organization operates—under the aegis of new thoughtware—automatically changes people's roles, and none is more crucial than when the senior management team goes off-line and allows the doers of the plan to become the makers of the plan. The doers are the ones who will successfully move the organization into the future—sorry senior management, but the reality is that you can't do it. Besides, it's no longer your role. Once senior management has articulated the case for action, they transfer the building of the evolution plan over to a representative, critical mass of people and take on their new role as "approvers" of the plan (when it is complete, and not until then). Senior management is *not* an integral part of the planning process. They have fulfilled their first obligation by providing the direction and goals (case for action), and now they must leave the "how to get there" to those that have to do it. This is a real rip at old thoughtware. It's not the traditional modus operandi where senior management leads the planning and is very involved in the process. This is strong, new medicine, and it takes a newly found discipline to carry it through. Many will find it difficult, and many will be inclined to cheat the process, to slip back into old thinking, and to try to be involved in the planning. *Don't do it.* Stay in your new role.

You have taken the first big step by removing the approvers from the making (doing), you have fulfilled your responsibility to this point by setting direction, and now you must wait for the process to evolve. These new roles might feel awkward at first, but they are very powerful.

Inherent in the new process, and made crystal clear to the builders, is the framework of responsibility that they now have, versus their previous roles. Now roles are described by *outputs*, not a list of activities in a job, and accountability is based on those outputs. In fact, there are four components of accountability:

1. Outputs—"What am I to do?"
2. Measurement—of specific objectives/performance. "How am I doing?"
3. Authority—clearly specified. "Am I allowed to do it?"
4. Skill set—adequately developed. "Am I able to do it?"

You cannot have allowment until these components are in place. Allowment puts information, skills, and authority at the point of variance *when* people are entitled, and when they have a clear line of sight to strategy. And in order to be aligned with the strategy you need to build a measurement system that navigates, not just evaluates. In turn, this requires education and skill development. These are the prerequisites for allowment to succeed. Only then, when these pieces are in place, can authority be released. Think about it.

In changing these roles, it often seems as if senior management is losing control, abdicating responsibility, and unleashing too much power to the people. In the old context this would be true, but in the new context what is in fact happening is *a harnessing of the power and a focusing of the thinking of all the people who actually make the organization run.* It is their role to determine how their organization will get to the future. They are the ones that make and break many of the "make or break decisions," every day. They hold the future, and the chance to get there, in their hands. They are building an evolution plan that exposes, clarifies, and solidifies. That's why the process is so important. That's why these role changes are critical.

One of the first, and most difficult, rules to abide by is that the content of the plan, and the recommended action, *is not open to senior management debate.* It's not their role. Their new role is one of approval, approval based on priorities and resources after the evolution plan has been completed. Their role is to complete the process by turning the evolution plan into a tactical vehicle which is sequenced and resourced so as to ensure that new thoughtware is installed, and that the redesigned, high-velocity organization is created in a quality and timely manner.

New Roles for the Management Team
- Provide clear vision, direction, and case for action
- Prioritize initiatives
- Allocate resources
- Measure progress
- Sponsor implementation teams
- Hold team leaders accountable
- Coach and protect the process

In the next chapter, we describe eight modules for installing the new thoughtware within this framework.

Notes

[1] C. William Pollard, *The Soul of the Firm* (New York: Harper Business, 1966). From Middlebury, VT: Soundview Executive Book Summaries, p. 1.

[2] Thomas Hout and John Carter, "Getting It Done: New Roles for Executives," *Harvard Business Review,* November–December 1995, p. 135.

Eight Installation Modules   **12**

He who has begun has half done.
Dare to be wise; begin!

—Horace, 65–8 B.C.

In this chapter we present eight modules for installing the new thoughtware and for implementing the new management process. Figure 12-1 diagrams the specific modules of learning and their application (the techniques). These modules follow a systematic sequence that creates a transition to the new management process. Table 12-1 summarizes the basics of each module. The different steps relate to the installation process discussed in Chapter 11 and depicted in Figure 11-3. Knowledge of the whole is captured in modules 1 and 2, measurement of what matters (creating tools for navigation) in modules 3 and 4, a focus on time to action in 5 and 6, and allowment (distributed authority) in 7 and 8.

Some organizations will begin with modules 3 and 4 (measurement), or with modules 5 and 6 (implementation of process improvement tools), but for allowment to occur, they

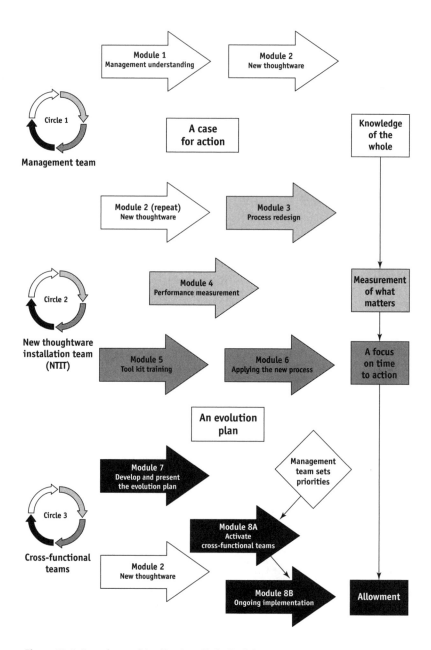

Figure 12-1. Learning and Application: Eight Modules

Table 12-1. Eight Installation Modules

Module	Who	What
1. Management understanding	All management personnel	Education on new thoughtware • Concepts and benefits • Project framework and resources • Methodology, tools, and software Decision making • Develop implementation plan • Identify members of the new thoughtware installation team • Develop case for action
2. New thoughtware (five days)	1. Management team 2. Installation teams 3. Cross-functional teams	Presentation of case for action Presentation of performance management hierarchy Education on techniques of new thoughtware
3. Process redesign (two to three weeks)	New thoughtware installation team (NTIT)	Relationship mapping training Analyze bottlenecks, variances, value-added processes Identify core, support, and management processes that impact case for action
4. Performance measurement	Management team and NTIT	Define performance ratio Define cost drivers Define hierarchy Build model First cut of measurement hierarchy

5. Tool kit training	NTIT	Ongoing workshops on how to apply education to processes
		• Process mapping • Cross-functional
		• Value-added • Cost/time/profile
		  improvement • Creativity
		• Identifying • Affinity diagram
		  bottlenecks

6. Applying the new process (two to three months)	NTIT	Collect data • Critical issues • Current processes • Identifying improvement projects • Align to measurement hierarchy • Document processes as they should be documented
7. Develop and present the evolution plan (six months)	NTIT	Presentation of evolution plan and completed measurement hierarchy • Current work processes • Plans to address evolution plan • Recommendation to activate evolution plan

continued on next page

Table 12-1. Eight Installation Modules (continued)

Module	Who	What
Management team sets priorities (one day)	Management team	Approve plan Set priorities Set measures Make tradeoffs for resource allocations Identify cross-functional teams
8A. The new management process: Activate cross-functional teams	Management team and NTIT	Train new membership in the new thoughtware and the tool kit Release evolution plan according to priorities set by management team
8B. The new management process: Ongoing implementation	All	Continually review priorities and add projects to evolution plan Hold the vision and maintain discipline in the new thoughtware

will have to return to modules 1 and 2 before proceeding to 7 and 8. The new management process, depicted by the shaded diamond between modules 7 and 8, will not be realized without full buy-in from the top, and without the understanding of new thoughtware throughout the organization. The organization cannot sustain the new thoughtware without the new management process to ensure distribution of authority horizontally and cross-functionally, and to set priorities for action on an ongoing basis.

Building the Case for Action with the Management Team

Articulating the company's strategic intent and case for action is senior management's mandate, and it requires the formation of a senior, cross-functional team that can take on this task. In Figure 11-3 (on page 210), the first circle represents this senior team. It must be totally cross-functional and go through two steps in preparing the organization's case for action. The two steps are depicted in Figure 12-1, and these precede setting forth the case for action.

Module 1: Management Understanding

Module 1 allows the management team to reach a clear understanding in a number of important areas. At this time they may go back and do some visioning, or revisit the organization's strategic intent, or put in more relevant measures before forming the case for action.

- Vision
- Strategic intent
- Commitment
- Measurement and motivation
- Consensus (of understanding)
- How to build the case for action

Module 2: New Thoughtware

In the new thoughtware module, the team acquires a strong understanding of the required new thoughtware. Here, there is new learning through simulation, workshops, and education that create a contextual shift—all customized to the organization's current state and desired goals. The senior team is immersed in new thoughtware on issues such as these:

- Flexibility versus efficiency
- Time versus price
- Solutions versus products
- Value-adding versus cost
- Internal flexibility versus external control
- Temporary versus permanent
- People as an asset versus people as an expense
- Navigation versus evaluation

The Case for Action

There is no typical case for action, but we have set out the general parameters of one company's case for action and the specifics of another organization's case for action.

A Case for Action Must First Be:

• A statement from a fully, cross-functional
  management team
• Clear
• Aggressive
• Actionable

Possible Parameters:

• Unacceptable working capital turns
• Complicated and ineffective process
• Intense departmentalization
• Complex financial management
• Creeping complacency
• Growing competition

Opportunities to Be Realized:

• Radically reduce elapsed time of delivery process (70–80
  percent)
• Substantially decrease inventory (50–60 percent)
• Eliminate non-value-adding activities and assets
  (75 percent)
• Reduce accounts receivable (35 percent)
• Increase asset utilization rate (to 125 percent)
• Measure employees by outputs in the process, not activities
  in departments
• Decrease capacity with current asset base
• Build a measurement model to navigate

Possible Limitations to Achieving the Case for Action:

• Resource availability
• Performance measurement alignment
• Too aggressive a plan
• Communications infrastructure
• Roll-out strategy
• Magnitude of effort and time
• Ingrained functional segmentation
• Programmatic mind-set
• Month-end realities

A Specific Case for Action

A manufacturer of railworks products has made quantum leaps ahead in only a year, with a challenging and ambitious case for action. Initially, they set out a specific, time-based objective of being able to go from order entry to shipping in 30 days. The company had regularly taken months and months to complete the cycle. In order to get there, they had to set out lots of specifics in their case for action. "We will build all castings in 20 days." "We will assemble all rail in 10 days." "We will enter all orders into the plant with full engineering information." "We will have 75 percent less paperwork." Now they have stretched that time objective to reach from customer request (going to get the information before order entry) to product at the customer's site, ready for installation, in *24 hours*. That's what adherence to a powerful case for action can achieve. The case for action generates a multitude of new thinking and identifies the areas of opportunity to be pursued. Figure 12-2 shows a typical breakdown of the areas where new opportunities can be found.

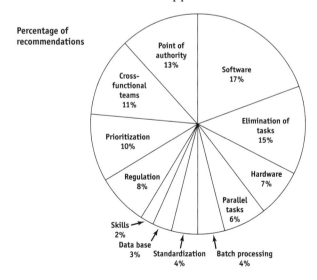

Figure 12-2. Typical Improvement Opportunities

Once the senior cross-functional team has developed the case for action, they present it to a larger body of cross-functional representation, depicted by the second circle in Figure 11-3 on page 210. We call it the new thoughtware installation team (NTIT). Their task is to build the evolution plan that can achieve the stated case for action.

Building the Evolution Plan with the New Thoughtware Installation Team (NTIT)

The new thoughtware installation team must be able to understand the scope of the entire process and it can require any number of people. Typically it constitutes about 3–5 percent of the total population of the company (second circle, Figure 11-3). Once the case for action has been handed off to this larger group, the cascading of momentum is in force, from which will emerge the evolution plan and the new process. This larger body, made up of any number of cross-functional teams, then goes through modules 2 to 7, in Figure 12-1, in developing the evolution plan.

Module 2 (Repeat): New Thoughtware for the Installation Team

The first step is the thoughtware module. Senior management has been through it, and now the NTIT must be fully cognizant of the imperative to shatter old thinking and prepare the groundwork for new thoughtware. Through simulation and new context workshops, the entire NTIT comes face-to-face with the impediments and dangers of the inherent, old thoughtware. They experience the difference between the old and new thoughtware, and prepare themselves, as a unified team, to move forward with a new understanding of what the planning process must address. They now realize how radically different—better—it can be, and they have common language and common thoughtware on which to operate. When senior management went through this module their focus was on strategic issues, whereas now the larger team has a tactical focus and gets into operational issues.

Module 3: Process Redesign

It is essential for senior management to establish up-front, clear parameters and sound process thinking with the NTIT because when they have completed the evolution plan they will have as many as a hundred or more actionable projects that they believe are necessary to achieve what is articulated in the case for action. So they need to have a common frame of reference as to what the organization is and how to build common purpose among a wide, disparate group of interests (from accounting to engineering to MIS to labor relations). Module 3 gets at building common purpose, common understanding, common approach, common knowledge—a common data base and platform of thoughtware.

First, there need to be common and uniform terms for all projects. We use the acronym SNIBECA in referring to the common outline of each. SNIBECA components are as follows:

• *Subject:* The subject defines the name and scope of the initiative. It can be stated as simply as "customer complaint/resolution system," or "revenue collection process." It should reference, however, a process or data map so that it can be viewed *in context.* The subject could be a statement of direction: "Optimize the order-entry process so as to reduce cycle time in the service delivery area," or "Develop a marketing data base in an effort to increase sales in Geography A."

• *Need:* This section should frame or define the problem or opportunity; for example, "The current (baseline) situation does not meet the cycle time requirements mandated in the case for action." "Salespeople and front-line staff do not have adequate sales tools to meet revenue targets." "Currently the market strategy is one of 'one size fits all' rather than process design of 'segment-specific strategies.'" The need may be very specific: "to reduce the average cost and time involved in the processing and payment of invoices." And the need should be really apparent upon the completion of this section.

• *Idea:* The idea addresses the question, "What can be done to solve or 'dissolve' the problem?" The idea may be a simple problem definition/solution or it may encompass a complete process design. For example, the idea may be "to localize responsibility for the order entry process from central office to branch offices," or "to develop a segment-specific program for each product group based on a customer needs identification study." These require further explanation as to how they would be done. Most importantly, the idea should respond directly to the section on Need. For example, the idea of "introduce a debit card system for field purchases" may impact the need of "increase working capital turns," but without further explanation the correction could be lost. Also, it is important to calibrate the ideas against the overall mandate as spelled out in the case for action.

• *Benefit:* It is important to spell out the benefits or consequences of the project in terms of how it closes the gap between baseline and entitlement. The benefit may be reflected in the performance hierarchy measurement system at a macro level—customer, financial performance, people quality, continuous improvement/innovation, or government and society. Alternatively, it may be easier to reflect the benefits at a lower cost-driver level such as on-time report accuracy, cash flow, inventory level, on-time billing/delivery ratio, etc. It is also useful to specify the results in terms of numerics: "An additional 300,000 hours of productive work power will be released," or "On a 2 percent revenue, growth can be realized by reducing order-entry cycle by three days."

Note that some benefits may be determined by either actual calculations or by some formula or explanation. For example, annual savings can be estimated based on industry customer retention rates: "A 2 percent retention rate equates to a 10 percent cost reduction." Benefits can be calculated by using available tools like cost/time profits. Also, benefits may be estimated from data bases: "It has been estimated that a 'debit card' can save a midsize company between $850,000 and $1.7 million annually." Benefits may also be measured in non-financial cost drivers such as value-added/non-value-added time, number of work days, number of transactions, etc.

• *Evidence:* This section calls upon all the data you have collected and translates it into the information required to give your idea merit. Evidence is readily available through the process maps, data maps, variance analysis, measurement hierarchy, cost-time profiles, interviews, etc., and other tools and techniques brought to bear on the redesign analysis. Examples of evidence may read "Current in-service cycle times for all products average 55 days and appear to be trending upward," or "56 percent of all complaints are related to our invoicing system," or "Our field offices receive 20,000 complaints per year," etc. Evidence is factual and anecdotal data to give the idea merit and validity.

• *Conclusion:* This should represent a statement of specific recommendations on how to access the benefits outlined above. The recommendation may reside on a continuum ranging from "the formation of a critical business issues team to work over the next six months" to "the reissuing of a policy statement immediately." For example, a recommendation could state: "Develop and utilize a standard installation information document that replaces existing forms in the current process," or "Investigate the process(es) currently used for handling survey information in order to provide a specific recommendation and design criteria for a complaint/feedback system that can be used in all locations." The former is a recommendation to act now, the latter is a recommendation to collect information. The conclusion could be as straight forward as, "Conduct a series of educational workshops," or as complex as, "Form a critical business issues team to report back on the feasibility of a new computer system." Again, the importance of the conclusion is in context of the case for action and its ability to close the gap between baseline and entitlement.

• *Action:* This is implementation. It should incorporate the following micro steps: (1) collate information by work group/product, (2) scan original directory and add new information, (3) sort and produce product directory, and (4) distribute and maintain electronically. It should also have some time frames . You might create a chart using months as time frames across the top; down the side you could list the following items as action steps: evaluate alternatives, liaise with suppliers, implement pilot, train all staff, start up. You should also estimate resource requirements. For example: a cross functional team will consist of 10 or 12 employees, the team will require about 400 work hours, start up to completion will take five months, and project will require 10K to do customer research and produce results. Then, there are very specific criteria for each project. These action criteria are project goal, tasks/activities, timetable, cost/benefit, measurement drivers, accountability, resource requirements, resource constraints, and red flags.

The SNIBECAs are a focused means that allow for common understanding and equitable comparison in the new prioritization and approval process; whereas, in the traditional management process, projects would be developed and approved in different departments, with different criteria, different resources, and different goals. And the results would be even more different, diffused, and disjointed than where they originated from.

Also in module 3, the NTIT is indoctrinated in *process thinking* as it applies *across* the organization. The new thoughtware module breaks down much of the old thinking, allowing the NTIT to direct the planning process across seven core business processes in the organization. All teams are built within, and according to, these core processes.

Seven Core Processes
- Strategic planning
- Demand generation
- New product development
- Distribution
- Supply
- Make-ship
- Customer service

Again, simulation is used to bring focus to what is a wide ranging, and expanding, cross-functional group. Through dialogue, provocation, simulation, and hands-on experience, the team builds a new and different relationship map that illustrates the complexity, and insanity, of how the organization currently operates. It is not the relationship map that matters so much as the process of creating it. A relationship map exposes the principles of process thinking and planning—*knowledge of the whole, management of white spaces, measurement of intangibles, removal of impediments to flexibility, and velocity,* and *the proper placement of information, authority and skills.* When they have finished this module, the whole NTIT sees and thinks about the organization differently—very differently. They now have an understanding of the whole and see the organization through its relationships and processes.

Module 4: Performance Measurement

Once process thinking becomes the modus operandi, then understanding, identifying, and measuring the real cost drivers becomes imperative. The team learns why *what gets measured gets done,* and how to develop activity-based measures that are vertically aligned and linked directly to strategies. And they learn new, non-financial measures. Simulation and software provide the team with a wide range of "what if" scenarios, which eventually are developed to create the new performance measurement hierarchy (discussed in Chapter 7). Senior management, in the case for action, will have identified major strategic issues and their corresponding goals. Now the NTIT has to tie the strategies and goals to meaningful, measurable activities. For example, customer satisfaction must be measured throughout the organization in such activities as order entry, on-time deliveries, returns, warranties, customer complaints, invoice accuracy, and so on. At this step, the NTIT also identifies all the activities that are drawing resources and driving costs in order to determine the common, across-the-organization values that are going to be measured. SNIBECAs are created to address these identified issues.

Quite often, in this module, a special team is created to develop new measurement thoughtware and software. They design the basics of a new measurement model and populate it with both qualitative and quantitative data representing the real process and cost drivers of the business.

Module 5: Tool Kit Training

The training in this module focuses on learning new tools, reviewing some old tools (cycle time reduction, inventory control, predictive maintenance, QCO, etc.), and *custom-designing all the tools based on the new thoughtware of the NTIT.* There are any number of tools available. Some are analytical, some descriptive, and some prescriptive:

- Process mapping
- Cost/Time profiles
- Baseline/Entitlement charts
- Information/Part flow analysis
- Activity-based costing models
- Overall performance measurement views
- Synchronous flow techniques
- Key variance analysis
- Continuous flow methods
- Pull system design
- Design for manufacturability
- Target costing and pricing
- Customer requirement work sheets
- Waste analysis
- Creativity techniques

- Role clarity
- Accountability descriptions
- Competency profiling
- Behavioral technology

Figures 12-3 and 12-4 show some examples of process analysis tools.

Module 6: Applying the New Process

With training complete and tools in hand, the NTIT moves through a sequence of applications in developing the form and content of the evolution plan. This includes:

1. Relationship mapping
2. Key variance analysis
3. Impediment and linear analysis
4. Calculating baseline and entitlement
5. Cost-time profiling
6. Creating SNIBECAs
7. Documenting the evolution plan

At this stage people start *doing,* even though the evolution plan has not been presented or approved yet. They're engaged in forming new teams, building cells, moving machines, plugging into networks, knocking down walls, and applying *new thoughtware.* At this juncture planning and enactment are simultaneous, and the actual application of the new process, in real time, is getting underway. By now there is a critical mass of people who have been participating in the new process (modules 2 through 5) and who are working with new thoughtware doing process redesign work, developing new measurements, and applying new tools.

Figure 12-3. Three Examples of Process Analysis Tools

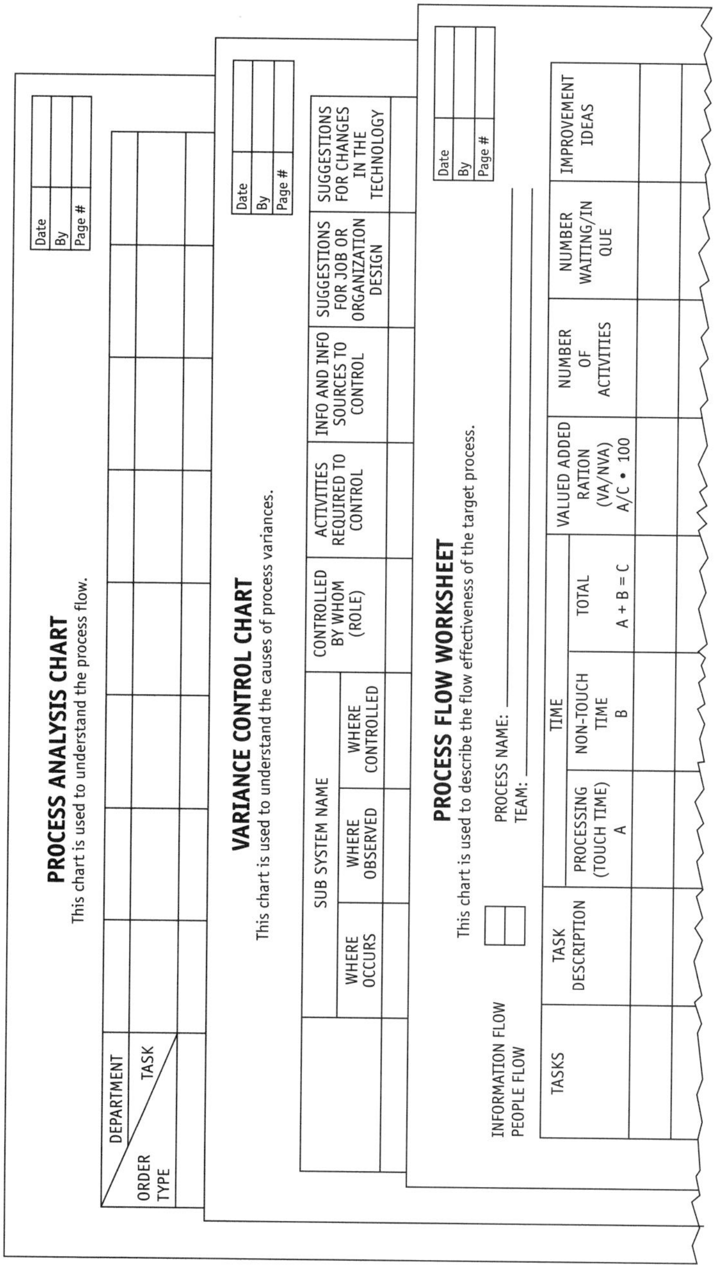

PROCESS ANALYSIS CHART

This chart is used to understand the process flow.

ORDER TYPE	DEPARTMENT / TASK					Date
						By
						Page #

VARIANCE CONTROL CHART

This chart is used to understand the causes of process variances.

SUB SYSTEM NAME			CONTROLLED BY WHOM (ROLE)	ACTIVITIES REQUIRED TO CONTROL	INFO AND INFO SOURCES TO CONTROL	SUGGESTIONS FOR JOB OR ORGANIZATION DESIGN	SUGGESTIONS FOR CHANGES IN THE TECHNOLOGY	Date
WHERE OCCURS	WHERE OBSERVED	WHERE CONTROLLED						By
								Page #

PROCESS FLOW WORKSHEET

This chart is used to describe the flow effectiveness of the target process.

INFORMATION FLOW ☐
PEOPLE FLOW

PROCESS NAME: _____
TEAM: _____

TASKS	TASK DESCRIPTION	TIME			VALUED ADDED RATION (VA/NVA) A/C • 100	NUMBER OF ACTIVITIES	NUMBER WAITING/IN QUE	IMPROVEMENT IDEAS	Date
		PROCESSING (TOUCH TIME) A	NON-TOUCH TIME B	TOTAL A + B = C					By
									Page #

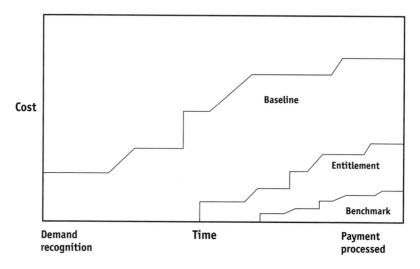

Figure 12-4. Cost-Time Baseline Entitlement Profiles

Module 7: Develop and Present the Evolution Plan

New thoughtware, process, tools, and real-time application lead to new, first-hand experienced change. A solid block of people (3–5 percent) from up, down, and across the organization sees and experiences the shift, and they are ready to set out the *must do's* (the projects) that need to be undertaken in order to meet the organization's case for action. It's a small revolution—within an evolutionary process. They present the *where we are,* the *where we must be,* and the *how we get there* in the evolution plan. It is a comprehensive series of actionable projects that must be realized if the evolving organization is to grow and achieve its goal.

The evolution plan provides the discipline so that nothing goes out into that environment and uses valuable resources that hasn't been released through due process. And although that due process is somewhat time-consuming at the beginning, by the seventh or eighth month it will become habit and quite natural. Each makes the commitment: I am not going to release projects within my own functional domain unless I can calibrate it against the other projects and draw resources from all over the company.

The presentation of the evolution plan is a unique creation in and of iteself. In many cases it has been done as a play. They are all unique. One play was so good the company wanted to take it on the road. Another company presented the evolution plan as a series of skits. A group of professors created a play for the rest of the faculty. There are many different ways of presenting the evolution plan, but using theater allows people to break old patterns of interaction with each other. It's also fun.

Module 8A and 8B: The New Management Process

Now the senior management team returns to the installation process in their new role. They begin by prioritizing the projects recommended in the evolution plan by the installation team. Revisiting the evolution plan, allocating resources, measuring results, and protecting the newly created process work constitutes their primary role in the new evolutionary organization.

The bottom part of Figure 11-3 shows a shift taking place in the organization from traditional management, through a transitional management phase, to an evolutionary management system. By the end of installation of the new thoughtware an organization will have initiated this new management process. The hierarchy remains but the roles have changed to focus on a different leverage point that allows a clear line of sight between management and the rest of the organization—horizontalism is established. Top management remains, at the end of the day, accountable for the overall performance of the business, but they have a more panoramic view. New measures are in place on learning, on customers, on internal processes, and on finance, and these allow senior managers to choose the top priorities for deploying resources into the future. This is their role. They will become involved in managing the projects directly at the operational level only when a project goes off spec. If a project falls behind or develops unforeseen difficulties the project manager can call in the management team. Generally, such problems will require adjustments in the allocation of resources, which is the appropriate arena for top management's involvement in the new management system.

This new management system allows the organization to sustain the new thoughtware, processes, and roles that have been installed. Ordinarily structural changes don't last in organizations because they are usually focused on expanding capacity. The whole purpose of this model is to ensure that it sustains itself by *forcing management to understand that the limitation they face is not a capacity issue but a priority issue,* and that the setting of priorities is a critical and powerful management tool. By the time installation reaches module 8, the priorities and how to measure them have been identified—once. But remember, this plan will be revisited several times. You will come back in a month and ask, How do your decisions look now? Do you want to change a priority, do you want to abort some, do you want to re-sequence them, do you want to take some out of inventory, put some back in? It is an ongoing process of evaluating priorities.

In evaluating the projects presented in the evolution plan the tendency will be to want to do them all. That is how most organizations have always lived. But with new thoughtware prioritization allows time. Decide what you won't do. In the beginning it usually becomes a forced comparison, calibrated against the goals of the organization (expressed in the case for action) and the leverage that each of the choices gives you toward that goal. You must always choose the higher-leverage projects.

Remember, SNIBECAs and the evolution plan are enacted in two ways, either through critical business issues teams (CBIT) or through rapid deployment teams (RDT), and it is management's role to drive the entire process by prioritizing and releasing projects to these teams. CBITs essentially put a plan together while RDTs enact the projects (often in a matter of weeks). Both need to be considered in an overall hierarchy of priorities. Prioritization does not have to be a complex process. It is much more of a dialog based around key considerations and questions. There are formal approaches such as *forced paired comparison,* or *nominal group techniques,* but we have found the basis for any prioritizing begins with a cross-functional dialogue aimed at answering a series of fundamental questions:

- Why does the organization need to work on this particular project? (For example, perhaps there are significant gaps between current level of performance and requirements.)
- Why does this process exist?
- What function does the process perform?
- What problem is being studied?
- What are the boundaries (starting and end points) for this project?
- Is there clear documentation of expectations? What is the magnitude of improvements required?
- Where does the project fit in the organization's overall improvement efforts?
- What is, and isn't, within the jurisdiction of the project?

- What limitations are on the project, including time and money?
- What are the beginning and completion dates?
- What authority does the project team have to call in co-workers or outside experts or to request information or equipment not normally accessible to them?
- Who is the sponsor? How often does the project team meet with the sponsor or guidance team?

This sets the basis for determining where any project fits in the overall priority hierarchy.

Since resources are already tapped out, managers have to decide what to tell people not to do in order to add this new capacity to their work load. Setting priorities becomes not just a word but a very tough job. In traditional structures, deciding priorities horizontally across the organization is rarely done. In marketing, packaging may be the number one priority; in finance, something else. In this model, *all functions determine together what the best use of resources is to be, and then each releases the necessary resources to accomplish that goal.* Finance adds resources to marketing's packaging project. Why would they do that? Because together they have come to the realization that by doing it this way there is much better leverage for the organization.

Most managers get pretty good at this, but some can't do it at all. If they can't get behind this, then sometimes their peers will hold them accountable. As well, the critical mass of understanding and the dialogue in the group will push these late-comers in the right direction. Throughout this process old assumptions are continually challenged as the new ones begin to kick in. The thinking is focused on the organization as a whole now, not on functional responsibility. People may still be thinking functionally—vertically—but the old model is starting to break down. Now, they are implementing horizontalism—stressing the priorities for the whole company. And knowledge of the whole supports this understanding and allowment emerges.

The decision point—the approval of the evolution plan in Module 8A—takes a day. You don't want to make this an onerous process. It has already been decided by the best people in the organization that this is what the company should do. If the management team takes three weeks to figure out whether it is the right answer or not, then you don't have allowment. It's best if the management team caucuses immediately after the NTIT's presentation and returns on the same day with their approval. The management team doesn't have to go away and study the presentation—they need to move on it. The installation team will come up with the best answer, and everyone knows it. They are the experts on this particular product or process or requirement; they live in it every day. They reached an agreement cross-functionally, so they have gone through due process, applied the proper tools, and articulated the proper question. How can their answer be wrong?

In Figure 12-1, module 8A—activation of the cross-functional teams—is the initial release of the evolution plan, and 8B—ongoing implementation of the management process—is the practice of revisiting it on an ongoing basis.

When allowment actually starts to kick in and when the management team starts to release the authority into the organization, a new level of training may be required in how to accept responsibility and authority and how to live and operate from a state of allowment. We all have spent our lives taking orders or giving them—operating from a single point of authority. Now we have to operate by influencing without authority. It is an entirely different skill set for everyone, not just managers. People who have never taken any initiative find it especially difficult. People will be put on teams who have no idea what the team is about and who think they shouldn't be there. They will not want to learn or be caught asking stupid questions. Sustaining the change will require people to live with uncomfortable behavior for quite a while. That is the essence of this phase. The rest of your life as an organization will be about getting better and better at that. Do the same thing and you are going to get the same results. If you want different results you have to learn how to *do* differently.

Creating Lifelong Learning

Remember the eight crucial questions in Chapter 10—the questions that are the footings in the foundation of new thoughtware? Lifelong learning was number eight. Without this crucial footing the whole platform of thoughtware will come tottering down into a heap of yet another failed change effort.

What does it mean to subscribe to creating a lifelong learning organization? It means continuously leveraging the human capability in an organization. Like anything else inside an organization, learning is a process. To be a lifelong learning organization you must have specific learning strategies and learning agendas. Perhaps two days out of every five weeks you don't go to your call center or work station but rather to a classroom or to work at a volunteer organization, or you stay home and read a book and write a book report. You do something that *manifests* lifelong learning. You build it into your structure.

The whole idea of the learning organization isn't about sharing experiences, it's about making an investment in human capital in order to survive. It changes reward systems from sticks and carrots to paying people for doing the job that is not being done at the moment. Thus, base salaries increase for knowledge accumulation, not merit accumulation, and operational performance is recognized in annual bonuses. There are many ways people can learn and contribute within a business: they can take charge of raw materials, they can learn how to run problem-solving sessions or how to read a balance sheet, or they can order all of the stationery for the company. Whatever it is, it's something that is outside the scope of their usual activities, something that gives them a bigger picture of the organization and helps shape the context in which they are working. There must be rigor in the commitment to learning for the people in the organization. You must systematically build learning into job descriptions so that people find ways to expand their own knowledge base within and outside the organization. The organization supports both. The expectation is that everyone is creating a learning environment of their own.

In a knowledge-based organization, where you pay people for learning and accumulation of knowledge, knowledge is the key ingredient that makes the organization more flexible. In a world where most companies have access to the same technology, continuous learning gives your company a competitive advantage. Ultimately, we want to reverse the ratio of operational activities to learning so that one or two days a week are for operations and the rest of the week is spent on learning. Learning must be recognized as the journey itself, the core objective of the organization, not a side task. And the structure of the organization must allow rapid deployment of that learning.

In our vision of a lifelong learning organization, jobs are performed by teams of people who are appointed to the team based on their knowledge in the field. When employees complete one job, they pack up their portable computers, grab their files, and join another team. The main asset they carry with them is their knowledge, and the manifestation of that knowledge will be in their selection to various teams. When employees need their batteries recharged, they take themselves out of play for a few months and go to the beach or stay home and read a few books or whatever combination works to keep individual learning the uppermost goal for the organization to support.

It is crucial to have a lifelong learning philosophy in place when management begins releasing authority into the organization—when allowment actually begins to replace the old thoughtware of a concentrated point of authority. Otherwise, how are employees going to learn the necessary skills to take initiative, to change, to adapt—to constantly rise to the challenges that a new thoughtware organization presents. To install new thoughtware without a commitment to lifelong learning is a waste of time. It would be like someone buying Darwin's *The Origin of Species* when they still read at a "Dick and Jane" level. The book might end up making a handsome addition to the bookshelf, but somehow it wouldn't be serving its real purpose.

The New Management Process | **13**

We are an intelligent species and the use of our intelligence quite properly gives us pleasure. In this respect the brain is like a muscle. When it is in use we feel very good. Understanding is joyous.

—CARL SAGAN
BROCA'S BRAIN

The presentation of the evolution plan is a turning point, a launching point, a platform, a point of no return. The process is in motion, a sizable number of people are committed, and the thinking has changed—*forever.* New thoughtware is installed, and now you need to make it available to the entire operation. What lies ahead is the opportunity to create an organization that is as adaptive, flexible, fast, and focused as it need ever be. It's now a matter of constantly expanding the new thoughtware and managing the new process.

Management Now Manages the Process

The evolution plan generates an effusion of projects and energy, and provides the fuel for the new process. Using the earlier metaphor that the organization needs to flow like a river, we can now see that the evolution plan is what primes the pump. Once the flow is started (the case for action ensures the right direction), it is continuous, flexible, and very powerful. The thinking, planning, and action are "in sync," implementation is continuous, and management now manages the process. They have four primary roles for which they are responsible, and these follow a natural sequence (see Figure 13-1).

1. Set priorities
2. Allocate resources
3. Measure and hold accountable
4. Coach and protect

Figure 13-1 sets out the framework in which the installation and ongoing implementation take place. It becomes a continuous and deeply imbedded discipline for managing the organization.

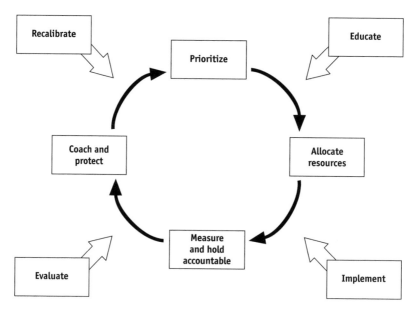

Figure 13-1. The New Management Process

1. *Set priorities:* The new evolutionary management process (Figure 13-2) differs significantly from the traditional management process (Figure 13-3). In the old way, many projects were approved and moved ahead, but there was no means of managing and continually prioritizing these projects; consequently, many eventually wandered, waned, withered, and died. The new process prevents this, as project approval is constantly subject to the new management process (Figure 13-1). Here you prioritize, resource, measure, and reconsider projects on a continuing basis—they can't wander and wither away. The new management process, by carefully and continually setting priorities, ensures that the organization remains aligned and focused.

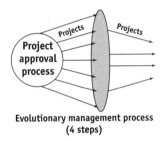

Figure 13-2. The New Evolutionary Management Process

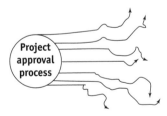

Figure 13-3. The Traditional Management Process

As shown earlier in Figure 11-3 (on page 210), the process is ongoing, continually releasing projects into the organization, acting on them, and putting others on hold until resources are available. Education about arising opportunities and how to identify these opportunities are crucial in making the best choices; consequently the new management process generates an environment that depends on continual learning.

2. *Allocate resources:* From the myriad of projects presented in the evolution plan the senior management team "approves for immediate implementation" those projects that they consider priorities. In conjunction with these priorities the management team must also allocate sufficient resources to ensure the projects can be effectively carried out. Then the teams implement either CBITs or RDTs (existing and newly formed teams as represented by the large circle in Figure 11-3).

3. *Measure and hold accountable:* In parallel to implementation, agreed-to measurements are established for purposes of evaluation and accountability. As projects proceed, they are monitored and evaluated relative to performance and against priorities (which often shift). Targets and measures provide the means to see the impact of your efforts on an operational level. They are tied to the health of the organization, to why you are doing what you are doing, and to who it impacts.

The most difficult, and most important, part of this process may be setting targets aggressively enough to force innovative solutions. In proposing projects to be implemented you must identify the problem, set challenging targets, and recognize the obstacles to achieving those targets. Without aggressive targets, people tend to leave things the same and just work harder or longer. In this mode, they can see the goal from where they are, but there is little reason to restructure the way they are doing things. When the targets are impossible to achieve within the existing process, teams revolutionize structure to achieve them.

4. *Coach and protect:* Throughout, it is management's responsibility to act as coach to the project teams and to protect the integrity of the process at all times. The latter responsibility often means protecting against creeping old thoughtware and tenacious old habits. In addition, management also builds links to systems, manages interdependencies, and aligns strategy and action through the measurement system. There is a built-in mechanism for recalibrating any or all facets of the process so you can change the priorities, resource allocation, measurements, or accountability in accordance with changing demand or circumstances.

Continuous Enactment (or Implementation)

Figure 13-4 depicts the implementation cycle as a continuous flow from the strategic to the tactical and from the tactical to operational implementation and then back to the strategic. At this stage, the three circles of installation shown in Figure 11-3 and described in Figure 12-1 and Table 12-1, have evolved into an ongoing, interactive, and cross-functional process among all three levels of the organization.

1. *Strategic:* From vision and strategic intent, the senior, cross-functional team determines the direction and critical issues to be addressed by the organization. These become the foundation for the case for action that provides direction for the new thoughtware installation team's tactical planning.

2. *Tactical:* From the case for action the installation team develops the evolution plan and submits it for prioritizing, resource allocation, and new measurement criteria. The senior management team then releases projects that best meet the

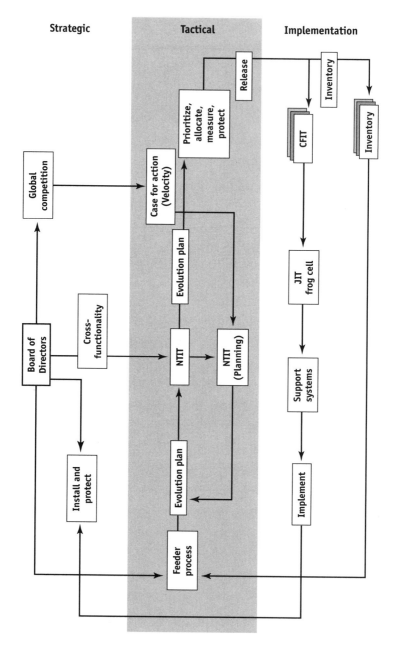

Figure 13–4. A Framework for Continuous Implementation

organization's case for action, priorities, and available resources.

3. *Implementation:* With the approved and released projects, cross-functional implementation teams move forward, new teams are formed, and implementation becomes an iterative process. You continually evaluate, complete, change, abort, and release new projects.

Within this overall framework the prioritization and resource allocation process provide the means for managing the process while new thoughtware drives the implementation process. You have complete enactment.

So What Happens?

The dynamics of the process generate extraordinary results, not the least of which is a collapsing of time. Change happens in never-before-considered time frames (Figure 13-5), participation and commitment reach never-before-imagined levels, and new thoughtware generates never-before-thought-of thinking *and* action.

Curve A: Typically, companies make many changes during the process of creating a product or service, before an order is entered (1). And after the order is entered changes continue, eventually diminishing as it nears completion. Even after shipping the order (2) some additional changes often are required. The process is very time-consuming and costly.

Curve B: The first step in getting faster is to reduce the time to order entry, the time to ship, and the number of changes being made after order entry.

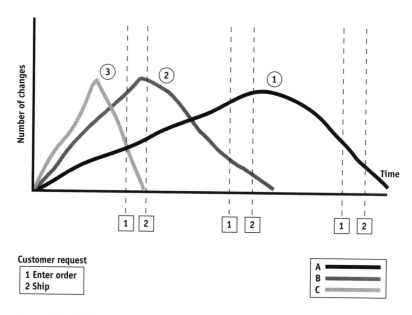

Figure 13-5. Getting Fast

Curve C: The objective is to compress the time frame to the point where when the order is entered there are very few changes, and by the time it is shipped there are no changes.

Time reduction is a key objective of the new management process and one of the critical factors in getting the organization on the right course to the future. However, there is much more to it than simply reducing cycle time.

The Components Are Everything

Figure 13-6 summarizes what we have been saying throughout this book and shows the relationship of the fundamental components to purpose, output, relationships, and participation. The installation of this requisite, cross-organization process cannot

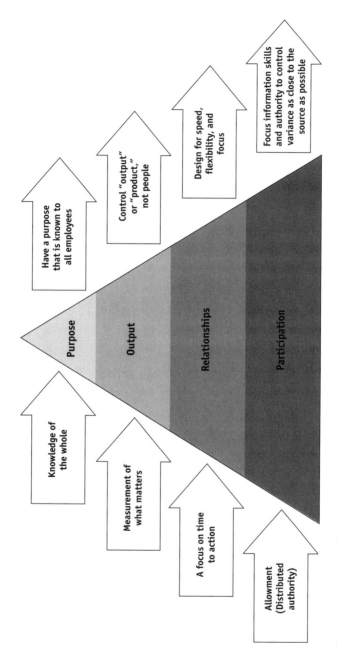

Figure 13-6. The New Thoughtware Drives the Organization

be done until there is a thorough, even visceral, understanding of the four fundamental components of the new thoughtware. This understanding must *first* be in place. Without it, the process—any process—will change very little, if anything.

Epilogue

*There is no expedient to which
man will not go to avoid the real
labor of thinking.*

—THOMAS EDISON

We've been into this change thing for years, some of us for a couple of decades or more. What with quality circles, JIT, Kaizen, TQM, ISO 9000, cycle time reduction, reengineering, restructuring, renewal, downsizing, right sizing, upsizing— and lots of capsizing along the way—we are drowning in all the change efforts. We are possessed by it. And the biggest obsession has been productivity, which has been pursued by many but achieved by few.

But the productivity obsession may be more of a virus than an antibiotic. Remember the facts: Despite the enormous investment in automation and computer technology, despite millions of layoffs intended to make us globally competitive, productivity increments have been few and fleeting, if at all. Productivity gains, in 18 industralized countries, during the period 1974–1992, have been only 40 percent of those made between 1961–1973 (0.9 versus 2.4 percent).[1] Also, sustainable change remains an endangered species. Moreover, much of the productivity gain has been made in quick-fix areas and support transactions, places that help make current numbers look better but that tell us nothing about the sustained capability companies may or may not have in the future. Endurance over the long haul, not short-haul bursts of strength (and share price), is paramount to long-term growth, and this comes from knowledge, ingenuity, and innovation, not simply productivity in processing.

> *In the race to the future, no one dares*
> *to fall a step behind, not nations*
> *or major corporations.*
> —WILLIAM GREIDER

At first glance, it makes sense to gain productivity by cutting labor costs and investing in technology. Besides, so many companies are doing it that no one can afford to slip behind; therefore, it's out with the people and in with the machines. The technology binge keeps getting bigger, faster, and cheaper every day. "[Information technology] now accounts for 41 percent of total business expenditures on capital equipment, making it easily the largest line item in U.S. corporations' budgets for capital spending."[2] This enormous expenditure and the equally enormous number of laid-off workers are the two prime ingredients in the productivity equation and the rationalization for the kamikaze approach to downsizing. But is it a well-founded justification?

Although downsizing has boosted short-term productivity and profits, it may have left in its wake a greater legacy: the inability to sustain growth. Will growth result from the massive cuts? The jury is still out. AT&T announced in November 1995 that it was letting 77,800 managers go;[3] in September 1996 the telecommunications giant indicated that "its third-quarter earnings would decline significantly from year earlier levels.... Now AT&T is saying its core business is weak, and that's alarming."[4] And only history will tell the full story and long-term price of Al Dunlap's romp on behalf of shareholders (of which he was one) through Scott Paper and Sunbeam.

As we await the verdict on downsizing, however, there is a mountain of evidence pointing to serious, long-range problems from mass layoffs that are destroying loyalty, job stability, and intellectual continuity—the very ingredients of sustained productivity. There's no argument that we've had to responsibly "trim fat" from our overweight, lumbering corporate Titanics. But it doesn't make much sense to dump thousands of crew overboard when it was primarily the captains and ship designers who got us where we are—not to mention the absence of accountability at the top. Now, we may be dealing with many empty corporate ships that can't compete because they do not have the intellectual capital that provides the invaluable core competency of a company.

It hasn't taken much cerebral exercise to figure out how to downsize, but it will take a great deal of forward, never-thought-of-before work to build an organization that is going to have the capability to handle the future—and stay there.

The Growth Imperative

"After two decades of exploding investment in computers, economists are confounded by the absence of any apparent pay off in productivity growth."[5] Today, more and more business leaders are recognizing that the productivity strategy is not working. There is a growing cynicism with the endless parade of programmatic, quick-hit prescriptions. The corporate dumpsters are full of what hasn't worked and the intellectual cupboards appear bare at a time when growth, and some kind of human renaissance, is desperately needed. We need a wrenching rethink.

The shift away from downsizing and a simplistic productivity equation toward *responsible sustainable growth* is the on-ramp to the autobahn of the 21st century. Every organization that is not yet in the fast lane must get there now. It's that critical. Every organization still working in the old structure, systems, and thoughtware of recent industrial times is destined to become roadkill. The fundamental old thoughtware, and the context it creates in our businesses, is way off track, and it keeps us going up the same old, wrong roads.

The new context demands sustainable growth, and sustained growth demands organizations that can *generate value over the long haul,* value not just for today's shareholders but for tomorrow's as well. This is not achieved by productivity alone. It comes by ensuring long-term demand for the organization's products and services. In fact, much of the voracious productivity we've been creating does just the opposite by eroding purchasing power (laid-off employees and stagnant incomes make for poor and fewer consumers), and eventually weakening demand with too much supply chasing too little demand. It's a vicious downward spiral—and that may be the most accurate definition of downsizing. Shareholders, boards, and management must realize that value and real growth only come when they move beyond the fixation on short-term earnings.

We already know a value-generating company must have certain inherent characteristics. It must be innovative, entrepreneurial, fast, flexible, focused, adaptive, market driven, customer obsessed, and creating not reacting. What we haven't figured out yet is how to create an organization that has the right genetic structure, capable of producing the required characteristics, capable of giving birth to a new organization that has these innate characteristics: vast, readily accessible, hands-on knowledge; comprehensive navigational and motivational measurements; natural speed and agility; and complete and unadulterated allowment. This is what changing the thoughtware is all about: *changing the very genetics of the organization.*

Many of today's organizations won't make it on the highway to the future. They can't because they are running on old thoughtware. They're like mainframes trying to keep up with a rising tide of PCs, laptops, and networks—it's all in the software. For organizations, it's all in the thoughtware. The core problem is that the basic thoughtware has not changed. And until it does, nothing much in the way of lasting growth and prosperity is going to happen.

Same Old, Same Old...

Don't bite into another program, don't keep changing content, don't throw more technology at it, don't keep banging on costs, don't keep cutting people. And don't keep reengineering and creating complete-process units, *if you're not going to change the context of the organization.* Neither the productivity nor the return is there (except maybe a return ticket to where you already are) if you don't change the context first. And new growth sure isn't there. What is there is more of the same—and we know it doesn't work. By installing new thoughtware, you will drive new thinking, create new context, unlock mind-sets, break down barriers, allay fears, change behavior, and change relationships. You will change everything that runs the organization. Nothing else can do it.

The Unthinkable

Let's stop kidding ourselves. If so much of what we've tried has been screamingly less than successful, then the problem goes all the way back to our thinking. That's where the buck stops. *What were we thinking?*

We believed in what we thought and we believed that what we did was right. History has shown that some of what we did was right, but what about all that has been wrong— not just wrong but off the mark, destructive, disastrous, and career-ending? What went wrong? The programs seemed good at the time. They made sense. They fit the problem. Some even worked initially. But for the price we paid, they should have been much better. How could so many programs, designed by so many, reviewed by so many, accepted by so many, be so wrong? It's unthinkable. Or is it just too mind-boggling to think that our thinking could have been wrong, so we don't deal with it at all?

Is it just in the thinking? Well, looking back, our thinking is the only thing we haven't fundamentally tried to change. We've changed programs more often than a pathological liar changes his story, but we've carried right on with the same old thinking. Oh, we've thought of new concepts, brainstormed new ideas, tried to get people to think about lots of new things, but have we ever really considered changing the massive inventory of precepts, assumptions, and givens on which our people operate every business day? In most cases, the answer is an unequivocal no. Why? *Because there has been no fundamental new thoughtware to enable the organization to undertake the daunting task of expunging old thinking and replacing it with something new and deeply central to human enterprise.* Without new thoughtware that can shift thinking, we have changed very little, and we remain mired in old context, watching history come at us like a recurring bad dream.

How Are We Going to Make It in the Future?

Of course we cannot predict the future. What we have may or may not fit in the future. What we do may or may not work in the future. What we know may or may not translate in the future. But, what we think *can* change in a nanosecond. And from our thinking we can fit, do, and learn whatever is required to make it as the future becomes the present. Our behavior, our actions, can change only if we change our thinking. To do this, we must have an abundance of new thoughtware to create the kind of organization that is being demanded by the future. We will *never* generate long-term prosperity with only a short-sighted investment in technology. That's like having hardware without software, and everyone knows that it's the software that really counts. Stretching the metaphor, it gives us nothing more than a hard-wired, technologically advanced organization with no new, operating thoughtware.

It's obvious we *must* invest in new thoughtware, new operating platforms, that become the foundation from which we generate knowledge, innovation, ingenuity, learning, and growth—all of which are capable of taking us into the far reaches of time. This means nothing less than a clear, intelligent, and responsible commitment to invest in our human capital, which is currently intolerably underutilized, underemployed, and undermined. Without a serious long-term investment in the genetic foundation of our organizations—the thoughtware—we will never leverage the true value inherent in our human capital. Without it, we will never change as fast as the rate of change itself, and if we can't even do that—you guessed it—history will repeat itself.

Notes

[1] "Productivity Paradox Puzzles Experts," *Wall Street Journal/Globe & Mail,* April 14, 1997, p. B1.

[2] Stephen Roach, "The Hollow Ring of the Productivity Revival," *Harvard Business Review,* November–December 1996, p. 85.

[3] "77,800 Managers at AT&T Getting Job Buyout Offers," *The New York Times,* November 16, 1995, p. A1.

[4] "AT&T Shares Dive 9.8% on Bleak Profit Outlook," *Wall Street Journal/Globe & Mail,* September 25, 1996, p. B10.

[5] "Productivity Paradox Puzzles Experts," *Wall Street Journal/Globe & Mail,* April 14, 1997, p. B1.

About the Authors

PHILIP KIRBY is a preeminent thinker in organizational design and sociotechnical systems of organizational behavior. His study of social dimensions and their interconnectedness with technical tools of organizational growth has led to the evolution of the theory of *thoughtware*. Philip has developed and applied this vanguard of thinking since the late 1970s and, today, counsels companies around the world on how to understand and install new thoughtware. Philip has a degree in Economics from Concordia University, Montreal, and a master's degree from York University, Toronto.

DAVID HUGHES is an intellectual partner of Philip Kirby's, a consultant, and a writer. After more than twenty years of senior management and consulting experience in strategic planning, organizational change, and the venture capital business, David now writes full time. In addition to two book projects with Philip, he has written a business novel that will be published in 1998. David has degrees from DePauw University, Indiana, and University of Western Ontario, London.

Books from Productivity Press

Productivity Press publishes books that empower individuals and companies to achieve excellence in quality, productivity, and the creative involvement of all employees. Through steadfast efforts to support the vision and strategy of continuous improvement, Productivity Press delivers today's leading-edge tools and techniques gathered directly from industry leaders around the world. Call toll-free (800) 394-6868 for our free catalog.

Building a Shared Vision
A Leaders Guide to Aligning the Organization
C. Patrick Lewis
This exciting new book presents a step-by-step method for developing your organizational vision. It teaches how to build and maintain a shared vision directed from the top down, but encompassing the views of all the members and stakeholders, and understanding the competitive environment of the organization. Like *Corporate Diagnosis,* this books describes in detail one of the necessary first steps from *Implementing a Lean Management System:* visioning.
ISBN 1-56327-163-X / 150 pages / $45.00 / Order VISION-B278

Building Organizational Fitness
Management Methodology for Transformation and Strategic Advantage
Ryuji Fukuda
The most urgent task for companies today is to take a hard look at the future. To remain competitive, management must nurture a strong capability for self-development and a strong corporate culture, both of which form part of the foundation for improvement. But simply understanding management techniques doesnt mean you know how to use them. You need the tools and technologies for implementation. In *Building Organizational Fitness,* Fukuda extends the power of his managerial engineering methodology into the context of the top management strategic planning role.
ISBN 1-56327-144-3 / 250 pages / $65.00 / Order BFIT-B278

Caught in the Middle
A Leadership Guide for Partnership in the Workplace
Rick Maurer
Managers today are caught between old skills and new expectations. You're expected not only to improve quality and services, but also to get staff more involved. This stimulating book provides the inspiration and know-how to achieve these goals as it brings to light the rewards of establishing a real partnership with your staff. Includes self-assessment questionnaires.
ISBN 1-56327-158-3 / 258 pages / $30.00 / Order CAUGHT-B278

Corporate Diagnosis
Setting the Global Standard for Excellence
Thomas L. Jackson with Constance E. Dyer
All too often, strategic planning neglects an essential first step and final step-diagnosis of the organization's current state. What's required is a systematic review of the critical factors in organizational learning and growth, factors that require monitoring, measurement, and management to ensure that your company competes successfully. This executive workbook provides a step-by-step method for diagnosing an organization's strategic health and measuring its overall competitiveness against world class standards. With checklists, charts, and detailed explanations, *Corporate Diagnosis* is a practical instruction manual. The pillars of Jackson's diagnostic system are strategy, structure, and capability. Detailed diagnostic questions in each area are provided as guidelines for developing your own self-assessment survey.
ISBN 1-56327-086-2 / 115 pages / $65.00 / Order CDIAG-B278

Do it Right the Second Time
Benchmarking Best Practices in the Quality Change Process
Peter Merrill
Is your organization looking back on its quality process and saying it failed? Are you concerned that TQM is just another fad, only to be replaced by the next improvement movement? Dont jump ship just yet. Everyone experiences failures in their quality improvement process. Successful organizations are different because they learn from their failure: They do it right the second time. In this plain-speaking, easy-to-read book, Peter Merrill helps companies take what they learned from their first attempts at implementing a quality program, rethink the plan, and move forward. He takes you sequentially through the activities required to lead a lasting change from vision to final realization. Each brief chapter covers a specific topic in a framework which leads you directly to the issues that concern your organization.
ISBN 1-56327-175-3 / 225 pages / $27.00 / Order RSEC-B278

Implementing a Lean Management System
Thomas L. Jackson with Karen R. Jones
Does your company think and act ahead of technological change, ahead of the customer, and ahead of the competition? Thinking strategically requires a company to face these questions with a clear future image of itself. *Implementing a Lean Management System* lays out a comprehensive management system for aligning the firms vision of the future with market realities. Based on hoshin management, the Japanese strategic planning method used by top managers for driving TQM throughout an organization, *Lean Management* is about deploying vision, strategy, and policy to all levels of daily

activity. It is an eminently practical methodology emerging out of the implementation of continuous improvement methods and employee involvement.
ISBN 1-56327-085-4 / 182 pages / $65.00 / Order ILMS-B278

Learning Organizations
Developing Cultures for Tomorrow's Workplace
Sarita Chawla and John Renesch, Editors
The ability to learn faster than your competition may be the only sustainable competitive advantage! A learning organization is one where people continually expand their capacity to create results they truly desire, where new and expansive patterns of thinking are nurtured, where collective aspiration is set free, and where people are continually learning how to learn together. This compilation of 34 powerful essays, written by recognized experts worldwide, is rich in concept and theory as well as application and example. An inspiring follow-up to Peter Senge's groundbreaking bestseller *The Fifth Discipline*.
ISBN 1-56327-110-9 / 571 pages / $35.00 / Order LEARN-B278

Secrets of a Successful Employee Recognition System
Daniel C. Boyle
As the human resource manager of a failing manufacturing plant, Dan Boyle was desperate to find a way to motivate employees and break down the barrier between management and the union. He came up with a simple idea to say thank you to your employees for doing their job. In *Secrets to a Successful Employee Recognition System,* Boyle outlines how to begin and run a 100 Club program. Filled with case studies and detailed guidelines, this book underscores the power behind thanking your employees for a job well done.
ISBN 1-56327-083-8 / 250 pages / $25.00 / Order SECRET-B278

Total Quality Portfolio
Strategic Direction Publishers (ed)
This powerful package, compiled from the work of many leaders in the total quality field, contains 17 briefing papers. Designed to give you a comprehensive overview of ideas like: zero Defects, Demings 14 points, the Shewhart Cycle, and Jurans trilogy, this portfolio will provide you with many new and exciting ideas. Gain a deeper understanding, through case studies, how to tie pay and rewards to quality performance, a 14-step approach to running your own quality audit, a self-assessment tool, and an entire section on the early warning signals for any Quality initiative in danger of costing more than it earns, most importantly, how to use the data you collect to create a powerful and effective company strategy.
ISBN 3-9520013-5-X / 6 Volumes / $295.00 / Order TQF-B278

The Unshackled Organization
Facing the Challenge of Unpredictability Through Spontaneous Reorganization
Jeffrey Goldstein

Managers should not necessarily try to solve all the internal problems within their organizations; intervention may help in the short term, but in the long run may inhibit true problem-solving change from taking place. And change is the real goal. Through change comes real hope for improvement. Using leading-edge scientific and social theories about change, Goldstein explores how change happens within an organization and reveals that only through "self-organization" can natural, lasting change occur. This book is a pragmatic guide for managers, executives, consultants, and other change agents.
ISBN 1-56327-048-X / 202 pages / $25.00 / Order UO-B278

TO ORDER: Write, phone, or fax Productivity Press, Dept. BK, P.O. Box 13390, Portland, OR 97213-0390, phone 1-800-394-6868, fax 1-800-394-6286.

Outside the U.S. phone (503) 235-0600; fax (503) 235-0909

Send check or charge to your credit card (American Express, Visa, MasterCard accepted).

U.S. ORDERS: Add $5 shipping for first book, $2 each additional for UPS surface delivery. Add $5 for each AV program containing 1 or 2 tapes; add $12 for each AV program containing 3 or more tapes. We offer attractive quantity discounts for bulk purchases of individual titles; call for more information.

ORDER BY E-MAIL: Order 24 hours a day from anywhere in the world. Use either address:

To order: **service@ppress.com**

To view the online catalog and/or order: **http://www.ppress.com/**

QUANTITY DISCOUNTS: For information on quantity discounts, please contact our sales department.

INTERNATIONAL ORDERS: Write, phone, or fax for quote and indicate shipping method desired. For international callers, telephone number is 503-235-0600 and fax number is 503-235-0909. Prepayment in U.S. dollars must accompany your order (checks must be drawn on U.S. banks). When quote is returned with payment, your order will be shipped promptly by the method requested.

NOTE: Prices are in U.S. dollars and are subject to change without notice.